The Royal Mile

Olof Koekebakker
Jacqueline van der Kloet

NAi Uitgevers/Publishers
Internationale Triënnale Apeldoorn

Contents

Foreword

Hanneke Toes

The Apeldoorn Triennial 2008 covers the broad range of knowledge and developments characteristic of the discipline of garden and landscape architecture. Within that very broad discipline, a thorough knowledge of plants is essential for a good plan. Knowledge not only of perennials but also of the application of shrubs and trees is called for, since living material cannot be summed up in catalogues. Only insight into how a plant grows and behaves will enable it to appear at its best.

There are only a few individuals who have completely mastered this field, both now and in the past. Who does not know the beautiful borders of Mien Ruys? Her enormous knowledge of plants, combined with her particular qualities as an architect, led to unique plans. The garden and landscape architect Hein Otto was also able to make very subtle use of different types within the settings that he designed thanks to his extensive knowledge of plants, always resulting in a splendid interaction between the architecture, the ecology and the composition of the different types of trees and plants. The designers of the Royal Mile also belong to this select group. Their designs make this book a source of inspiration for those who love plants and apply them in their surroundings, a source of inspiration for both the garden lover and the professional responsible for the design of greenery in the public space.

Many would very much welcome a border design like the Royal Mile in their own town or village. As the interviews show, however, this type of planting calls for intensive maintenance. That means that an application of this kind is only possible on a limited scale. Urban greenery, however, is not only determined by the greenery in public space, but above all by that in gardens. The garden is still the ideal spot for beautiful plant borders. That is why I hope that the visitors, too, will be inspired to plant more perennials in their gardens and thereby to make a luxuriant contribution to the appearance of the public space. I am sure that visitors to the Royal Mile and readers of this book will become enthusiastic about the potential of the interaction between perennials, annuals, biennials, bulbs and corms to enhance the environment in which they live.

Hanneke Toes
Chairperson, Netherlands Association for Landscape Architecture (NVTL)

ist's impression of the Royal Mile, 2007

The Royal Mile

Jacqueline van der Kloet

There are those commissions whose content cannot be entirely pinned down beforehand. In the autumn of 2005 I was invited to design a border more than 1.5 km long for the first Apeldoorn Triennial. The objective was described as 'a Royal Border 1609.34 metres long (with the ambitious name *The Royal Mile*) designed by a number of the best border designers in the Netherlands and abroad'. The Royal Mile was to be one of the most colourful and florid parts of the Triennial. Given its international character, a form would have to be found to achieve the desired result with several border specialists from the Netherlands and further afield. It would be a unique way of working for the Netherlands. I was seized by conflicting feelings of panic, excitement and euphoria, leaving me with the realization that this might well be one of the most exciting commissions ever. In the end I did not need to think about it for long. You are not asked to be main designer and curator of an unusual project like this every day.

In making a vegetation design, you usually start with the location and its shape, but in this case the procedure was exactly the opposite. The plans for the Triennial already contained a picture of what this enormous border should look like. All that still needed to be done was to find a location where it could be implemented. The plan for the Royal Mile was elaborated in close collaboration with the Environment, Mobility and Public Space Department of the Apeldoorn Local Authority, where Jos van Nuenen was appointed as coordinator. I was to spend many hours with him in his capacity as technical adviser, negotiator, and not least pro and stay.

Our first concern was to find an appropriate location. It was no easy task, for where do you find a piece of land in the locality more than 1. km long that you experience as a single long strip, without its being obstructed by traffic features and buildings, and with enough light? After considering various locations, we found the almost perfect spot in Berg en Bos Park. I is the Jubileumlaan, which leads to the Apenheul, and its continuation, a path through the woods that gives access to the scenic area on the west side of Apeldoorn. A striking deta is that the Jubileumlaan is the exact spot where a big memorial event took place in 194 on the occasion of the golden anniversary of the reign of Queen Wilhelmina. That event, 'Flowers in Berg en Bos', was such a success that the formula was repeated down to 1955. Afterwards, the borders beside the Jubileum-laan were kept tidy and occasionally a new shrub or a group of perennials or seasonal

Jos van Nuenen, coordinator of the Royal Mile

...een Wilhelmina and the Princesses Juliana, Beatrix, Irene and Margriet visit the
...ibition 'Flowers in Berg en Bos', Berg en Bos Park, Apeldoorn 1948

...nts were added, but without any attempt to
...n with the surrounding landscape and
...hout any internal coherence.
...the summer of 2006 it was high time to
...ide on the composition of the vegetation.
...nting the strip over its full length with
...ennials would be too expensive in view of
...temporary nature of the project (three

months in the summer). Besides, with at most
one interim growing season in 2007, we were
actually already too late. After all, the average
perennial border takes time to reach maturity.
In the first year the plants have to take root,
after which they develop in the second growing
season, before appearing at their best in the
third year.

The alternative was a border with temporary vegetation, but that would require enormous quantities of plants and would therefore involve a lot of expense. The impasse was broken when the Apeldoorn Local Authority expressed the desire to have something to remember the Royal Mile by after the Triennial. It was decided to lay out the first part, from the main entrance of Berg en Bos Park to where it widens (the Acaciaplein) with perennial borders. The second part, beside the woodland path, would be filled with a one-off combination of flowering summer annuals and summer bulbs.

We focused first of all on the perennial borders, which would already have to be planted in the spring of 2007. It is quite a challenge to create an image that can rivet attention over a length of 400 m. At the same time we had to make sure that the borders would harmonize with the atmosphere in this part of the park: not too cultivated because of the woodland setting, but with a certain decorative value. After all, they line an important route for walkers.

The basic design was deliberately kept simple so that the emphasis would come to lie on the variegated composition of the planting. The principles were:

- Grass strips, 1 m wide, run parallel with the boulevard and demarcate the borders at the front.
- The borders themselves are 4.5 m wide: two strips of plants, each 2 m wide, separated by a path 0.5 m wide for maintenance.
- In the first part of the Jubileumlaan the wood forms the background on the left-hand side. The décor on the right is determined by the Theehuis. In the second part – after the pergola, which dates from the original laying out of Berg en Bos – tidily clipped beech hedges demarcate the borders at the rear.

Some of the original shrubs (various types of hortensia and viburnum, a few magnolias and a

Perennial border plant list

Shrubs
Buddleja davidii 'Nanho Blue'
Euonymus alatus
Hydrangea arborescens 'Annabelle'
Hydrangea macrophylla 'White Wave'
Hypericum kalmianum 'Gemo'

Higher and/or solitary perennials
Agastache 'Blue Fortune'
Anemone hybr. 'Honorine Jobert'
Anemone hybr. 'Königin Charlotte'
Anemone hybr. 'Whirlwind'
Chelone obliqua
Echinacea purpurea 'Magnus'
Gillenia trifoliata
Geranium sylvaticum 'Amy Doncaster'
Helleborus viridis
Kalimeris incisa 'Blue Star'
Kirengeshoma palmata
Lunaria rediviva
Pennisetum alopecuroides 'Hameln'
Phlox paniculata 'Blue Evening'
Solidago rugosa

Ground-covering perennials
Alchemilla mollis
Brunnera macrophylla
Brunnera macrophylla 'Jack Frost'
Calamintha nepeta 'Blue Cloud'
Carex morrowii 'Ice Dance'
Deschampsia cespitosa 'Tatra Gold'
Dicentra formosa 'Langtrees'
Euphorbia amygdaloides 'Purpurea'
Euphorbia amygdaloides var. robbiae
Euphorbia cyparissias 'Fens Ruby'
Geranium hybr. 'Philippe Vapelle'
Geranium macrorrhizum 'Czakor'
Geranium macrorrhizum 'Ingwersen's Var.'
Geranium macrorrhizum 'Spessart'
Geranium magnificum
Geranium oxonianum 'Rose Clair'
Liriope muscari
Molinia caerulea 'Overdam'
Omphalodes verna

pical plants in the perennial plant border: Japanese anemones and blue phlox, autumn 2007

perennial plant border after a design by Jacqueline van der Kloet, autumn 2007

ouple of Japanese maples) were kept or moved elsewhere in the new plan. They structure the borders, and since some of these shrubs flower in the early spring or have an attractive silhouette in the winter, they give the borders an atmosphere at a time when most perennials are resting. These plants are set in very natural-looking borders whose composition matches the woodland atmosphere. Since the situation in the borders is like the one they have come from, they will do well here.

Perennial honesty, Japanese anemone, various types of geranium, euphorbia and Caucasian forget-me-not, which all grow well on locations that are in semi-shade, will complement and support one another wonderfully. Here and there they alternate with types that have been chosen for the sunnier spots. Aniseed, cone flower, basil thyme and other types of geranium do well together here and combine to form an attractive variant of the shade assortment.

The selection of types has been determined by various characteristics to ensure flowering over the largest possible number of months. We have also chosen types with an attractive leaf (all year round where possible) and types that offer an attractive picture not only during flowering but also afterwards, thanks to their foliage, decorative seed pods and attractive autumn and winter silhouette. Because there are so many different decorative properties, there will something to see practically all year round.

Within the borders, taller plants stand out that emerge from a carpet of different groups of ground cover, intermingling in a more or less arbitrary fashion. Sometimes these taller varieties are single plants, sometimes they form groups that infiltrate other types here and there.

Anemone x hybrida 'Honorine Jobert'

Since a large part of these borders is in the shade or semi-shade, pastel tints have been chosen to brighten up these darker areas: white, cream, yellowish green, light blue and pink. In the parts with more light the composition is in a brighter yellow, pinkish red and purple-blue. Some combinations of plants are repeated, but always in a slightly different way, to create an exciting rhythm.

If the plants develop optimally, they will require relatively little maintenance, which is a big advantage in a semi-public space.

By the beginning of April 2007 the vegetation plan was ready, and a nurseryman was found who could supply the unusual assortment within a couple of weeks. It looked as though supplying types such as perennial honesty, Blue Paradise phlox (a new variety) and green hellebore (*Helleborus viridis*) was going to cause problems, but in the end the Rijnbeek nursery in Boskoop managed to deliver them all on schedule.

Planting took place in June and during one of the warmest weeks in the year, between 18 and 25 June, I had to do my very best to keep ahead of the planters. I was probably one of the few who did not at all mind that it was followed by a period of prolonged rainfall. The plants shot up, and so did the weeds, which were cleared by hand every week by the Berg en Bos maintenance department so as not to damage the tender roots of the young plants. The success of this approach was revealed in September. The ground cover had already formed an almost closed carpet and the taller perennials had grown considerably. The white Japanese anemones (*Anemone hybrida 'Honorine Jobert'*), which flowered until November, were particularly admired.

During those months I also worked hard on the content of the second part of the Royal Mile. This was the part that would receive the lion's share of attention in 2008 - not least because of its international character.

The basic design was ready by the beginning of June 2007. As in the area with the perennials, long straight borders 4.5 m wide would be created on either side of the path, but here they would be directly adjacent to the path. The total length was divided into two times five borders, each roughly 70 m long. The composition of each of the ten borders would be up to one of the ten designers. Since the path runs more or less in an east-west direction, the borders on the right-hand side are in almost uninterrupted sunlight. Bright colours are at their best in a location like this. It was decided to progress from dark to light colours: from purple via bright red, bright orange and bright yellow to white.

The light is less bright on the left-hand side of the path. The borders here are in pastel tints, because these colours are better in the half-shade. Matching the colour progression on the right-hand side, the tints pass from lilac via pink, pastel orange and pastel yellow to grey-green. The picture I had in mind was of borders that look like ribbons of flowers with a very natural character, as though you are walking through a gigantic meadow of flowers which surprises you at every turn with its changing colours and shapes. The idea was to stun the average visitor with the pure pleasure of seeing so much beauty. At the same time we wanted the Royal Mile to provide inspiration not only for interested garden-lovers, but also for the planners of urban greenery. They can see here what can be done on a larger scale with colours and shapes, so that they will hopefully be inspired to apply it to the environments for which they are responsible. By now I had also started to invite the group of border designers and vegetation specialists from the Netherlands and abroad. When I had taken part in a symposium on planting in Freising,

Germany, in 1995, I had got to know a number of colleagues who all shared a passion for planting. The group met again in the Netherlands in the following year. We decided to form 'Perennial Perspectives', an international foundation for the promotion of the use of perennials, especially in public greenery. In the succeeding years the members of the group continued to meet, often on the occasion of a planting event, but also socially, and the result was a tightly knit association that now proved its worth.

By the end of June 2007, the definitive list of designers had been drawn up. Each of them was enthusiastic and determined to make a fine contribution. Of course, a visit to the location was essential, so the whole group came to Apeldoorn for two days on 24 August. Jos van Nuenen gave a presentation on the Triennial and Berg en Bos Park in particular, after which I gave the designers more specific information. According to my concept, the borders should contain a combination of summer annuals and flowering summer bulbs. Almost all annuals have a period of flowering lasting from a few weeks to several months. Bulbs flower for a shorter period, but they provide a strong accent. In theory there should be at least 10 per cent summer bulbs and a maximum of 90 per cent flowering summer annuals, but the designers could play a bit with those percentages.

The second condition was intended to keep the succession of colours in the borders visible. At least half of the plants must flower in the main colour of the border concerned; the rest could be filled in as the designers chose. Each of them was allocated a colour during a hilarious drawing of straws, and after some lively swapping the result was as follows:

• **Purple border:** Wilko Karmelk and Helen Lewis, garden designers and owners of the Ferdinandushof nursery in Overslag (Zeeland Flanders). They have been experimenting in their model gardens for years with perennials, annuals, and spring and summer bulbs.

Red border: Christopher Bradley-Hole (UK) in collaboration with Anita Fischer (Germany), both garden and landscape architects. Christopher Bradley-Hole has won many prizes at the Chelsea Flower Show with his garden designs, Anita Fischer organizes the annual 'Freisinger Gartentage'.

Orange border: Jane Schul (Denmark), landscape architect. She is specialized in combinations with annuals. Jane Schul is also chair of the Royal Danish Garden Society.

Yellow border: Julie Toll (UK), garden designer. She too has won various gold medals at the Chelsea Flower Show. Julie Toll is specialized in combinations which include wild plants.

White border: Ursula Gräfen (Germany), landscape architect and lecturer in planting at the Weihenstephan Fachhochschule.

Lilac border: Jacqueline van der Kloet (the Netherlands), greenery designer who has been working for more than 25 years with combinations of perennials, annuals and flower bulbs. She experiments with them in her own garden: De Theetuin in Weesp.

Pink border: Eric Ossart and Arnaud Maurières (France), garden designers. Ossart and Maurières are fascinated by combinations with flowering summer annuals. Their first work was to be seen in the city of Blois and at the festival of Chaumont-sur-Loire. By now they have commissions for public vegetation all over France.

Soft-orange border: Fleur van Zonneveld (the Netherlands), garden designer and owner of the garden and nursery De Kleine Plantage in

c design for the Royal Mile by Jacqueline van der t, June 2007

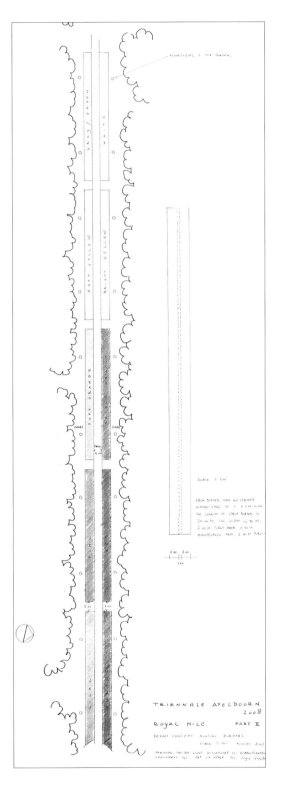

Eenrum (Groningen) for the last 25 years. Through experimenting on her own terrain she has built up an enormous knowledge of perennials and unusual annuals.

- **Soft-yellow border:** Christian Meyer (Germany), landscape architect. He often collaborates with Christine Orel. They are both passionate plant lovers and use their knowledge mainly for large-scale combinations of perennials and seasonal plants. Their work could be seen at the 2001 'Bundesgartenschau' in Potsdam, the 2003 'Internationale Gartenbauausstellung' in Rostock, and elsewhere.
- **Greyish-green border:** Christine Orel (Germany), landscape architect.

All of the lists of plants were at the nursery on 15 October 2007, which then faced the task of producing a total of 38,000 annuals. For logistical reasons it was convenient to grow all the plants on a single location. Through my wor for the Efteling amusement park, where I desig ed various borders with spring bulbs for the main entrance and along the main route, I had got to know a firm with the space, time and experience to be able to take on a project of thi magnitude. Ed Oomen and his daughter Joyce from the Overaa nursery in Breda are specialize in cultivating fantastic annuals and biennials, which is why they are often asked to supply theme parks and local authorities in the Netherlands and abroad. They are constantly looking for new selections and regard the Roya Mile with its unusual types and varieties as a big challenge.

For the summer bulbs I approached the Inter-national Flower Bulb Centre, for which I have been working for years. The centre promised t sponsor a large part of the 4,500 bulbs and al helped us to find a nurseryman who could hav them ready for planting. Usually, summer bulb are planted as dry bulbs from the end of April. The earliest that they will flower is in July, depending on the weather. If you want annual and summer bulbs to grow together, however, is advisable to plant the bulbs as young plants with roots at the same time as the annuals, fr mid-May. Willem Heemskerk from the Davelaa nursery in Woudenberg was prepared to pot the bulbs, and as a specialized cultivator of crocosmias (known by some under the name Montbretia) he promised to sponsor all the crocosmias used in the plans. The organizatic

Dahlia 'Thomas Edison'

...it to location in August 2007 with (left to right): Christopher Bradley-Hole, Jacqueline van der Kloet,
...vid Gobaut, Christian Meyer, Fleur van Zonneveld, Wilko Karmelk, Ursula Gräfen, Jane Schul, Julie Toll,
...en Lewis, Vivien Millet, Anita Fischer and Christine Orel

...nt more smoothly than I could have dreamed. ...he meantime the local authority was not ...ing idle either. The landscape architects Linda ...ijer and Han Goudswaard, who have been ...olved with the renovation plans for Berg en ... for some time, shared their thoughts with us ...how to deal with a number of spots that form ...t of the Royal Mile. To start with there is a ...dification of the Acaciaplein, which is the link ...ween the two parts of the Royal Mile. It marks ... transition from the central park area to the ...ds behind it. The Acaciaplein has been

given an oval shape, emphasized by a beech hedge with niches for wooden benches with illumination from below. There was also a need to give the Royal Mile a clear finishing point, so the end of the borders with summer flowers was marked by a wooden construction: a small tower that is positioned asymmetrically in the boulevard. It is a landmark in the wood, a point to head for, and from which to look back on the borders and the adjacent woodland meadow from a great height. After the Triennial, the tower will be dismantled into two parts which

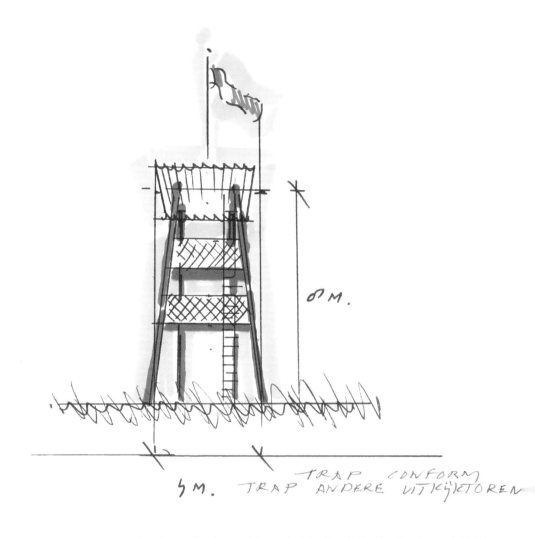

TRAP CONFORM
TRAP ANDERE UITKIJKTOREN

5 M.   0 M.

Design sketch for the wooden observation tower at the end of the Royal Mile, Han Goudswaard, 2007

will be used as viewing huts near the deer meadow.

By February 2008 the borders were ready for planting and technical features such as a fence to keep out wild boar were well under way. The planting of all the annuals and summer bulbs began on 13 May. It was a very difficult task logistically, because the idea was to plant two borders a day without getting in one another's way. A schedule was drawn up to ensure that the two borders planted each day were as far as possible from one another.

Almost all the designers were present on the spot to supervise the planting of their border.

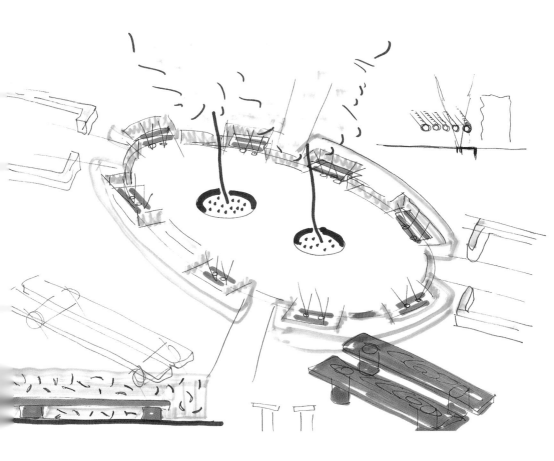

'gn sketch for the oval Acaciaplein, Han Goudswaard, 2007

n then on weather is the only unpredictable
or. Everyone hoped for plenty of sun with the
sional shower. Thanks to an anti-weed layer
gned by the Overaa nursery to cover the
nd, weeds are given barely a chance and the
ers can develop optimally.

certain that visitors from near and far will

come to Apeldoorn this summer for a spectacle
of colour that has never been seen before in the
Netherlands.

*Jacqueline van der Kloet, main designer and
curator of the Royal Mile*

The Royal Mile

Wilko Karmelk
Helen Lewis

Jacqueline van der Kloet

Ossart & Maurières

Fleur van Zonneveld

Christian Meyer

Christine Orel

Wilko Karmelk

Helen Lewis

Christopher
Bradley-Hole

Anita Fischer

Jane Schul

Julie Toll

Ursula Gräfen

Wilko Karmelk
Helen Lewis

'A range of purple tones from light lilacs to powerful purples are mixed together with shades of orange, red and white. Elements of contrast appear throughout the border in use of colour, flower and leaf shape. Silver-grey foliage plants accentuate the dark mysterious purples. Plants like *Perilla frutescens var. 'Nankinensis'* act as focal points at certain intervals with their purple spiky foliage.

Bold plants such as *Nicotiana sylvestris* and *Cynara scolymus 'Violetta di Chioggia'* add dramatic impact with their large leaves. Selected grasses like *Briza maxima*, *Hordeum jubatum*, and *Pennisetum massaicum* diffuse and blend the colour palette.

Verbena bonariensis and *Allium sphaerocephalon* are woven throughout the border, creating a natural ambiance in this array of vibrant and colourful plant combinations.'

Wilko Karmelk and Helen Lewis

nineteenth-century Beervelde Park near Ghent, where the well-known Beervelde Garden Days are held twice a year.

Their love of and talent for garden design onl really emerged after they had decided to lay out a number of model gardens for their nursery. Those gardens enable visitors to the nursery to see the fully-grown plants and can offer them inspiration for ways of using and

Ferdinandushof, the company of Wilko Karmelk and Helen Lewis, is situated in Zeeland-Flanders, barely a 100 m from the Belgian border. They started it as a perennial nursery, but over the years the design of gardens and borders has become an increasingly important part of their work in addition to the cultivation of plants. By now they no longer confine themselves to private gardens, but also carry out projects on a larger scale in parks and on estates. One of the most striking of these is the double English border that they designed for the

Borders in Overslag in natural planting style, July 2007

combining them. 'Visitors were enthusiastic about how we had laid out the gardens and one thing led to another. We started to design small gardens for private clients here and there. Now we also take on large assignments.' Various mixed borders of perennials and shrubs can be seen in situ at Ferdinandushof. There is also a sunken garden with

an emphasis on grasses, and a colourful Mediterranean-style garden with many exotic plants.

Those exotic plants are a particular favourite of Wilko Karmelk. As a boy he was already collecting and cultivating plants, and every time he went to England to view the gardens there, he almost always came back with a few exotic plants. When he rented his first plot of land at the age of 18, he already had a large collection of mainly perennials. In the end he was able to make a profession of his passion. His partner Helen Lewis took a design course in England and worked for five years as a designer in London. Then she met Wilko and moved to the Netherlands 15 years ago. Since then they have formed a team. She says that her design background has stood her in good stead, particularly for presentations: 'I'm always interested in how things come across.' They can always agree pretty quickly. For the Royal Mile they began by each drawing up a list of plants. After that they looked at ways of combining those lists. They turned out to have both chosen the same main plants. 'If we make a list like that, we think about the structure as well as the colour. Dahlias, for instance, have fairly big flowers, which go well with flowers that have a finer structure. Other plants have lovely greyish-silver leaves. We were delighted with the colour purple that we had drawn and with a border that receives full sun.'

To make a border of the considerable length of 70 m manageable, they divided it into three sections. Each section contains more or less the same plants, but they are grouped differently in each one. The purple plants

Beervelde double border, Park van Beervelde, Belgium, September 2006

Wilko Karmelk, Amsterdam,
the Netherlands, 1964
Helen Lewis, Oxford, England, 1962
Live and work in Overslag
www.ferdinandushof.nl

provide continuity. When the first design was ready they sketched in the purple with tracing paper. This enabled them to see how it flowed through the border. They then modified the design at the points where the purple did not yet link properly.

Wilko: 'We like to work with contrasts of form and colour. We are doing that at the Triennial too. To contrast with the purple we are using orange, for example – a warm colour which is easy to combine with. To make the border more natural we have interwoven other plants here and there, including grasses. This gives the border a composition from low to high.'

Wilko and Helen organize various theme days in their nursery in the course of the season, starting at the end of January with the Hellebore Days. In May there are the Open Garden Days, and in July the Dahlia Days. They invite other specialized nurseries to take part. In the summer they hold the Mid-summer Plant Fair, including lectures, with 30 colleagues. Some people return every year. The visitors come from everywhere: not only from the Netherlands and Belgium, but also from France, England, Luxembourg and Germany.

Their nursery activities are not limited to familiar plants. If it is at all possible, they take the opportunity to develop new variants. Sometimes they find an unusual plant in the garden, for example a random hybrid, and then they keep it for propagation. The plants are first kept in isolation for a year to see how they develop.

A favourite plant is the dahlia. Helen: 'Dahlias are rewarding plants. They flower from July to the first frost. We like late-bloomers which you

Beervelde double border, Park van Beervelde, Belgium, October 2007

can still enjoy in October and November.'

Wilko: 'There's a sort of dahlia revival going on. It's plain to see during our Dahlia Days in July.'

Wilko Karmelk and Helen Lewis do a lot of selection work in the case of the hellebore. They pay attention not only to the colour, but also to the shape of the flower: only those plants with regular, round flowers are kept. Usually they have a particular purpose in mind, for example a flower with one colour on the outside and another on the inside. But it sometimes takes generations of cross-breeding and sowing to achieve that.

Plant list

Annuals

1. Ageratum 'Red Sea'
2. Angelonia 'Dark Lavender'
3. Briza maxima
4. Bupleurum rotundifolium
5. Calibrachoa 'Orange Glow'
6. Cleome spinosa 'Helen Campbell'
7. Cleome spinosa 'Queen Violet'
8. Cosmos bipinnatus 'Sensation Albatross'
9. Cuphea lanceolata 'Purple Passion'
10. Cynara scolymus 'Violetta di Chioggia'
11. Erigeron karvinskianus
12. Gaura lindheimeri 'Whirling Butterflies'
13. Gilia tricolor
14. Helianthus annuus 'Ruby F1'
15. Helichrysum petiolare
16. Heliotropum arborescens 'Marine'
17. Hordeum jubatum
18. Lathyrus odoratus
19. Lavatera maritima
20. Leonitis nepetifolia 'Navajo Apricot'
21. Lobelia 'Hadspen Purple'
22. Nicotiana knightiana 'Green Tears'
23. Nicotiana sylvestris
24. Nicotiana 'Tinkerbell'
25. Nigella papillosa 'African Bride'
26. Pennisetum massaicum 'Red Buttons'
27. Perilla frutescens var. 'Nankinensis'
28. Persicaria orientalis
29. Salvia horminum paars (S. viridis)
30. Salvia 'Purple Majesty'
31. Salvia splendens 'Salsa Purple'
32. Scabiosa atropurpurea 'Black Knight'
33. Tagetes 'Linnaeus'
34. Tithonia rotundifolia 'Torch'
35. Verbena donalense 'Lavender Grace'
36. Verbena bonariensis
37. Verbena rigida
38. Zinnia tenuifolia 'Red Spider'

Bulbs

39. Allium sphaerocephalon
40. Cosmos atrosanguineus
41. Crocosmia 'George Davison'
42. Dahlia 'David Howard'
43. Dahlia 'Karma Naomi'
44. Dahlia 'Scura'
45. Dahlia Thomas Edison'
46. Dahlia 'Twilight Time'
47. Liatris spicata 'Kobold'

The Royal Mile

Jacqueline van der Kloet

Jacqueline van der Kloet

Ossart & Maurières

Fleur van Zonneveld

Christian Meyer

Christine Orel

Wilko Karmelk

Helen Lewis

Christopher Bradley-Hole

Anita Fischer

Jane Schul

Julie Toll

Ursula Gräfen

The Lilac Border

Jacqueline van der Kloet

'Lilac is absolutely not my favourite colour, far from it, but by chance lilac was assigned to me and I had to do something with it. The disappointment I felt at first soon became a challenge and gradually I discovered that lilac, which I always thought to be sweetish and bland, is a colour you can do exciting things with. Lilac as a colour becomes more solid when it is supported by darker tints from the same segment of the colour circle, such as violet-blue and purple. And a combination with pink is only successful when mixed with daring colours such as bright-red and orange.

Finally, as always, here too a catalyst is needed. This is found in neutral grey, deep-red and the regular green of plant leaves and ornamental grasses.

My favourite way of planting, everything mixed in an orderly manner, is used here as well, resulting in a casual plant scheme which remains fascinating to look at for weeks on end.'

Jacqueline van der Kloet

If you leave the densely built-up inner city of Weesp via the narrow bridge over the River Vecht, you find yourself in a different world. The island of the former Fort Ossenmarkt is largely green. That is particularly true of the northern part, where De Theetuin is situated: a flower and plant garden owned by Jacqueline van der Kloet that is open to the public. The studio where she makes her planting designs is located above the tearoom. 'During my training in Boskoop I met two young men with whom I stayed in contact after we had finished the course. We often travelled together to look at gardens. We discovered the phenomenon of gardens that are open to the public in England. It hardly existed in the Netherlands at the time and we thought it was a great idea to start something like it here – linked to our work as garden and landscape architects. It would enable us to show the kind of gardens we had in mind on our own site.'

They discovered via an advertisement from the Estates Department that the Bakker-schans bastion in Weesp – which had been abandoned years earlier by the Ministry of Defence – was for sale. When they went to view the property, all that could be seen was narrow path; the rest was covered with weeds.

Top: De Theetuin, Weesp, July 2007
Bottom: Schloss Ippenburg, Bad Essen, Germany, June 2007

34

The Efteling theme park, Kaatsheuvel, the Netherlands, April 2007

2 m high. It had accommodated a small nursery until 1963 which used to supply the barracks of North Holland with summer annuals. The greenhouse was still there as well as a number of cold frames, which they could naturally put to good use. When the envelopes of the potential buyers were opened, the trio turned out to have made the highest bid. The project to turn the complex into an attractive garden, including homes for the three families, took a further three years. De Theetuin opened in May 1986.

At about the same time Jacqueline van der Kloet had decided to venture on a career as an independent designer. This would enable her to concentrate entirely on planting. 'I had worked for six years with a company in Amsterdam, and planting was generally a secondary affair there. We did a lot for housing associations, and they had no money for unusual trees and bushes. It was only when I started to concentrate more on private gardens that I discovered what an enormous range of plants there was and what wonderful things you can do with them.'

In that early period she found an important source of inspiration in Gertrude Jekyll, the British garden architect who designed a lot of gardens on estates in the south of England around 1900. 'Jekyll worked in a very free and natural way, with a focus on perennials. Every time I visited one of her gardens, I always came home full of ideas. Since then that free style of designing has been a constant feature of my work.'

Perennials are her big favourite. 'Because they are so dependent on the seasons, they keep changing all year round. Later I fell for bulbs too; they show you that spring is back. The more you look into them, the more new types and combinations you find.' When she started out as an independent designer she mainly did private gardens. The more large-scale commissions, such as the Keukenhof and the Efteling, came later. When Piet Oudolf was commissioned to design the vegetation for two parks in the USA (Battery Park in New York and Lurie Garden in Chicago), Jacqueline van der Kloet assumed responsibility for a complementary plan for spring bulbs. And recently she drew up a plan with Julie Toll, who is also participating in the Royal Mile, for a park in Gotenburg that will open this year. This regular collaboration with fellow designers goes back to the 1990s, when an international group of professionals under the name Perennial Perspectives held regular meetings. Jacqueline van der Kloet wrote columns at the time for *VT Wonen* and for one of them she interviewed Piet Oudolf on *Astrantias*. After she had been talking to him

Jacqueline van der Kloet
Deventer, the Netherlands, 1950
Lives and works in Weesp
www.jacquelinevanderkloet.nl

all day, he asked whether she would be interested in going with him to a symposium in Germany. A small group of them travelled around there for a week, and they organized a symposium in the Netherlands in the following year. 'That's how Perennial Perspectives was born, with Rob Leopold as the driving force. Rob was also the one who expressed the vision of Perennial Perspectives in a unique way. That vision was based on our conviction that the quality of greenery in the public space was disappointing. We wanted to show with examples that a lot more could be done with public greenery using perennials.'

The colour that Jacqueline van der Kloet drew for her border on the Royal Mile is lilac. 'I've kept the design simple. I use three main sorts for the structure: the *Verbena bonariensis*, the *Pennisetum villosum*, and the *Salvia greggii*. The first is very tall, but does not block the view. The *Pennisetum* is an ornamental grass about 15 cm high, and the *Salvia* is a bush with small bright red flowers. I've also looked for colours to tone the lilac down a bit, such as green grass with white tufts, or a plant with a greyish leaf. So the contrast is with four plants with strong colours: the bright purple *Verbena*, two orange *Crocosmias*, and that red *Salvia*. The lilac is strengthened through that play of attraction and repulsion, toning down and heightening.'

Only the main structure is determined in advance. The rest of the plants will be planted on the spot. She thinks that is the best way to achieve a natural effect. You see a continuous picture, but with a higher and a lower level. The latter is supposed to become a kind of carpet after a few weeks. The higher plants, which also grow sideways, emerge from it. It will therefore look very different at the end of July from how it looked at the end of May. It must keep looking good until September - not just thanks to the flowers, but also through the structure and form.

The Keukenhof, Lisse, the Netherlands, April 2006

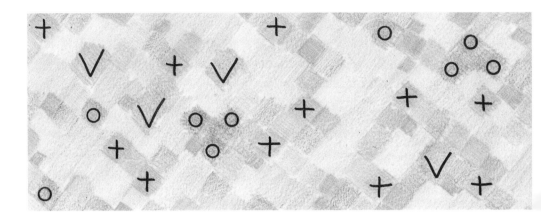

Plant list

Annuals

1. Ageratum houstonianum 'Leilanii Blue'
2. Coleus scutellarioides 'Palisandra'
3. Gaura lindheimeri 'Siskiyou Pink'
4. Helichrysum petiolare 'Silver'
5. Pennisetum villosum
6. Salvia greggii 'Royal Bumble'
7. Scaevola hybr. 'Esmeralda'
8. Stipa tenuissima 'Pony Tails'
9. Verbena bonariensis
10. Verbena rigida

Bulbs

11. Crocosmia 'Emily McKenzie'
12. Tulbaghia violacea 'Silver Lace'

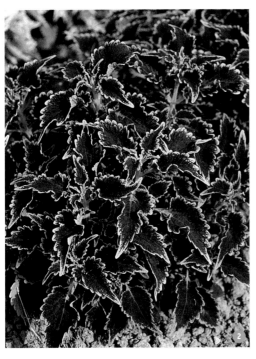

The Lilac Border

Jacqueline van der Kloet

The Royal Mile

Christopher Bradley-Hole
Anita Fischer

Wilko Karmelk

Jacqueline van der Kloet

Helen Lewis

Ossart & Maurières

Christopher
Bradley-Hole
Anita Fischer

Fleur van Zonneveld

Jane Schul

Christian Meyer

Julie Toll

Christine Orel

Ursula Gräfen

Christopher Bradley-Hole
Anita Fischer

The Red Border

'This border is inspired by the idea of a meadow discovered in a field of sunflowers. Another inspiration is the work of the English painter, Howard Hodgkin, and in particular his use of intense colour and the characteristic way he paints the frames of his pictures as well as the canvas.

The result is an abstract composition, not a literal interpretation. The sunflowers here are red rather than the more typical yellow to emphasize the artistic inspiration. Blocks at each end of the border act as 'bookends' which announce the start of the red border and create the frame for the pattern within. Further into the border the sunflowers are gradually inhabited by other plants which form a stylized meadow of mostly red flowers emerging from a background of grasses and the white flowered umbellifer, *Ammi majus*.

The meadow has a similar character throughout – an informal matrix, but at points it is punctuated by a wave of the blue flowered *Phacelias* which creates a sharp highlight in among the red flowers in the way that a block of strong colour occurs in a painting by Hodgkin.'

Christopher Bradley-Hole and Anita Fischer

Christopher Bradley-Hole occupies a clear-cut position in the world of garden architecture. He refers to himself as a modernist and is convinced that the role of modernism in garden and landscape design has by no mean been fully played out yet. He sees contempor ary design as a constant search for new idea instead of following established patterns. 'There is no standard way of making a garden I start afresh with every commission.'
He recently published a book on the subject, *Making the Modern Garden*, in which he explains what he regards as the most important characteristics of the modern garden. One of these is abstraction vis-à-vis nature; another is working with grids and enclosed spaces. If the use of new materials and technologies is added, an arsenal of possibilities is opened up. 'The way one material meets the other and the detail of

Top: Crockmore House, Henley-on-Thames, Oxfordshire, England, September 2001
Bottom: Pavilion Bury Court, Bentley, Hampshire, England, August 2002

Stone amphitheatre, Newick, East Sussex, England, August 2003

that meeting can be wonderfully expressive,' he says.

Another modern characteristic is the way that the spaces flow into one another. One of his great examples is the Barcelona pavilion by Mies van der Rohe, which actually consists of a series of walls that never quite meet. 'There is a suggestion of rooms, but they are implied rather than enclosed. This feeling of space flowing through the composition, and the hierarchy in the design, some spaces expressed as being more important than others – for me that captures the spirit of modernism.'

Within this modernism, Bradley-Hole has a predilection for minimalism. His book *The Minimalist Garden* was a bestseller. 'In minimalism everything is reduced to pure form. By taking out all the unnecessary things,

you can make something incredibly powerful. There is a great beauty in something that has really been reduced to the essence.'

Christopher Bradley-Hole does not just draw inspiration from an architect like Mies van der Rohe, but his own roots are in architecture too. 'As a child I enjoyed gardening, but when I had to choose a profession gardening was not on the radar. I think I'd never even heard of landscape architecture. My background was more likely to lead to my becoming a lawyer, stockbroker or architect.' He chose architecture because it satisfied his urge to design. After completing his studies he worked for years as an architect. He became a partner in a large firm and later started up his own architectural practice with two associates in Covent Garden.

Two factors precipitated the major volte-face

Christopher Bradley-Hole
Brighton, Sussex, England
Lives and works in London
www.christopherbradley-hole.co.uk

His interest in gardens took off in a big way when he started to design a garden for himself. At about the same time his passion for architecture had somewhat cooled, mainly because his work as an architect had become more and more commercial. 'I imagined how wonderful it would be if I could make a living by designing gardens.'

It was around this time that *Gardens Illustrated* announced a design competition for the Chelsea Flower Show. 'This is my chance,' he thought, and decided to enter. What was almost his first garden design was the winning entry. That set a train in motion that has never stopped since.

Bradley-Hole has thus never had any formal training in garden design; he picked up his knowledge of plants along the way. 'I was like an obsessive convert. I was ravenous for information from all quarters. I read whatever I could get my hands on, I wanted to know everything about every plant I bought. I also learnt a lot by visiting specialized nurseries. That is how I developed a substantial knowledge of plants. My lucky break came in 1995 when I met the Perennial Perspectives group. I suddenly got to know a lot of colleagues there, with the great Dutch garden philosopher Rob Leopold as the cohesive factor.'

Bradley-Hole designs both private gardens and public parks. He likes the combination. Private gardens afford an opportunity to experiment, whereas in public spaces there is more pressure to get things right in one go; it is not easy to make changes afterwards. Vice versa, he acquires experience in public commissions, for example with constructional details, that can come in handy in designing private gardens.

After the successful first time, Bradley-Hole has taken part in the Chelsea Flower Show on five subsequent occasions. He has won five gold medals and twice the prize for the Best Show Garden. He was supposed to take part again this year, but has postponed it for a year. 'We don't have enough time at the moment and I want it to be absolutely perfect again. It has to be a special minimalist garden – and nothing is worse than a minimalist garden that is just not quite good enough.'

He created the design for the Royal Mile together with his German colleague Anita Fischer, whom he met at Perennial Perspectives and with whom he regularly collaborates. The concept is a meadow with grasses and summer flowers, with blocks at both ends consisting of red sunflowers that enclose the meadow like two bookends. Most of the summer flowers are red too – that is the colour that they chose by picking straws. There are flowers of another colour to form a contrast, such as *Phacelia*, which is a strong blue flower.

Christopher Bradley-Hole: 'An important source of inspiration for this concept were the paintings of the British artist Howard Hodgkin. One of the interesting aspects of his work is that he paints over the frame too. In a certain sense you can regard the sunflower bookends as the frame that we're painting over. It wasn't our intention to make a literal copy of a Hodgkin's painting, but thanks to his inspiration it's become a sort of Howard Hodgkin meadow in a frame of red sunflowers.'

Until a few years ago, the vast majority of commissions that Anita Fischer generated were from government or public institutions including projects such as school grounds, kindergartens and crèches. This has changed in the last four or five years. Once she had been given the opportunity to design a number of beautiful gardens, one commission followed the next. Today, three-quarters of her work consists of private gardens.

At the start of her career Anita Fischer was not very interested in designing private gardens. 'I grew up in a politically committed family, so designing the environment in which people live and work was always very important to me. I have done a lot of work on children's surroundings, as well as hospitals, council homes and even cemeteries. From the cradle to the grave, you could say.'

But now she finds designing private gardens more rewarding. Appreciation of gardens has been growing in Germany. People who ask you to design their gardens now understand that compared to building a house, a garden is never finished and with a careful and constant maintenance it gets better and better over the years

There is yet another factor that makes designing private gardens attractive. 'You can communicate directly with the user. If you design a new school ground, you often don't even know who the principal will be, let alone knowing the children. During the design process one has to deal with experts from different departments, who certainly know their job, but sometimes are not informed of the children's needs. Many of her private clients have become good friends. Now and then she travels with them, for instance to Piet Oudolf's nursery or to Chelsea Flower Show. It would not be uncommon for them to drive back to Germany with a van full of plants.

Anita Fischer received a thorough training. 'In this profession you have to know about plants. We were drilled in an almost pedantic way. We had to learn everything about plants and it certainly wasn't always fun. But when I look back I have to say that we were given exactly the right tools.' After her studies she often found it restricting to design with plants following the tough guidelines of her teachers. Then she started to travel a lot, especially to England and the Netherlands, to find out about different approaches.

With her wide range of international contacts she became the German representative of Perennial Perspectives, a group of plant specialists who regularly organized exchange and symposia on perennials in the 1990s. 'We

Private garden, Munich, Germany, May 2007

The Red Border

Anita Fischer

introduced our more scientific approach to planting design; an approach based on plant sociology and the ecological requirements of herbaceous plants developed by Prof. Richard Hansen. As the result of his research at the famous Trial Garden of Weihenstephan, founded in 1947, perennials were categorized according to their natural habitats: woodland, woodland edge, open ground, rock gardens, border perennials, water's edge/marsh and water. This approach enables us to create sustainable planting schemes with reduced maintenance requirements.'

Anita Fischer met Christopher Bradley-Hole at the first Perennial Perspectives symposium. Since then they have collaborated on a series of projects. 'We understand each other's approach very well and there is a nice combination of design and technical expertise. Through the exchange of ideas (many of which are rejected) a surprising, and better, result can emerge'.

That's how they worked on their design for the Royal Mile. It was a challenge for Anita Fischer because she usually does not work with annuals.

'The colours of the different borders were drawn by lot. Red was our colour. It soon became clear to us that the border should have a meadow-like character and so we began the design by listing the red flowering annuals we both liked and also plants which would help us to create a meadow-like planting scheme.

But it mattered a great deal to Anita Fischer that it should be more than a meadow. 'Since naturalistic meadows are very fashionable these days, I thought that it needed something extraordinary. After considering various possibilities, Christopher came up with the famous work of the English painter Hodgkin, where the frames are part of the paintings. That's how the design emerged. Anita Fischer feels that with increasing experience she gained independence in her design work. 'I like precisely defined spaces and straight lines. The big advantage of working with plants for me is that they add softness and naturalness to the strong structures. That contrast of plants hanging over straight edges is very attractive and so the design does not need any winding lines. In my designs I like planting fruit trees in accurate grids in lush natural meadows. They provide not only the beauty of the blossoms and shade but also fresh fruit, which people tend to appreciate more and more today.'

The hard materials Anita chooses depend entirely on the nature of the project and the genius loci. 'Well and carefully designed, steel and concrete can be beautiful. But I am also very fond of natural materials like stone, gravel and wood. Now and then I visit quarries to find the right stones for my designs. We often use one stone in different shapes and sizes and according to function and design with different surfaces.'

A fine knowledge and understanding of both hard materials and plants is for her crucial for good design quality.

Anita Fischer
Traunreut, Germany, 1960
Lives and works in Freising
www.freisingergartentage.de

The Royal Mile

Private garden, Munich, Germany, May 2007

otanic Garden, Munich, Germany, 2005

The Red Border

Christopher Bradley-Hole
Anita Fischer

Plant list

Annuals

1. Ammi majus 'Graceland'
2. Ammi visnaga 'Green Mist'
3. Antirrhinum majus 'Black Prince'
4. Antirrhinum majus Liberty Crimson
5. Centaurea cyanus 'Black Ball'
6. Cosmos bipinnatus 'Dazzler'
7. Cosmos bipinnatus 'Pied Piper Red'
8. Helianthus annuus 'Claret F1 Hybride'
9. Helianthus annuus 'Prado Red'
10. Helianthus annuus 'Velvet Queen'
11. Juncus pallidos 'Blue Arrows'
12. Juncus pallidos 'Javelin'
13. Juncus ensifolius
14. Lupinus polyphyllus 'Edelknaben'
15. Nicotiana 'Green Tears'
16. Papaver somniferum 'Burgundy Frills'
17. Papaver somniferum 'Hens and Chicken'
18. Pennisetum setaceum
19. Phacelia parryi 'Royal Admiral'
20. Scabiosa atropurpurea 'Ace of Spades'
21. Scabiosa 'Chile Black'
22. Verbena bonariensis

Bulbs

23. Cosmos atrosanguineus
24. Dahlia 'Arabian Night'
25. Dahlia 'Bishop of Auckland'
26. Dahlia 'Nuit d'Été'
27. Dahlia cactus 'Nadine Jessie'
28. Dahlia 'Chat Noir'
29. Dahlia 'Hollyhill Electra'
30. Dahlia 'Night Queen'

The Royal Mile

Ossart & Maurières

Jacqueline van der Kloet

Ossart & Maurières

Fleur van Zonneveld

Christian Meyer

Christine Orel

Wilko Karmelk

Helen Lewis

Christopher Bradley-Hole

Anita Fischer

Jane Schul

Julie Toll

Ursula Gräfen

The Pink Border

Ossart & Maurières

'Green and pink are colours that go well together naturally. A special harmony can be found in the particular combination of different varieties of ornamental tobacco plants, for example between the deep pink and lime green varieties. They are scattered over the border at random, but in such a way that a homogenous picture emerges.

During the season the castor oil plants (*Ricinus*) become more distinct. They are planted in diagonal lines across the border, resembling a botanical choreography. They grow as quickly as weeds and might almost acquire a bad reputation on that score, but fortunately we have opted for the special pink variety *Carmencita*.

It has a marble-coloured leaf with a variety of shades of pink, green and grey. The large number of fruits that appear in the course of the summer are reminiscent of lychees. In September we could pluck armfuls and turn them into enormous bouquets by adding some green flowers. This reveals the design's inspiration: a bouquet to guide the selection of plants for this ornamental border.' *Ossart & Maurières*

It was more or less practical considerations that led Eric Ossart and Arnaud Maurières to start their design career with ephemeral gardens – gardens destined for a short lifespan. After completing their studies, neither of them wanted to work first for a large firm, so they decided to start out by themselves right away. Since they had no experience, they did not immediately receive commissions for real gardens, but concentrated on exhibitions. Japanese exhibitions were very popular in the 1980s and they soon became specialized in artificial Japanese gardens that were dismantled again after a week or a month.

Eric Ossart: 'The attractive thing was that it did not take much time to create such ephemeral gardens. We saw right away what

Top: Jardin Noria, Gard, Saint Quentin-la-Poterie, France, summer 2007

Bottom: Hôtel de Cluny (Musée national du Moyen Âge), Paris, summer 2007

The Pink Border

*Bedeau of Deduit, Anglards-de-Salers, France,
autumn 2007*

worked well or not. In the case of ordinary gardens there is often a long period between the initial ideas and the implementation, and then it still takes years for the plants to develop.'

In the 20 years or so that have passed since then, their work has moved in a number of directions, but they have always cultivated thinking in terms of the ephemeral.

The success of their Japanese gardens took Ossart and Maurières to Blois, a city beside the Loire south of Paris, where they were eventually to establish their practice. Jean-Paul Pigeat, an important figure in the field of modern art, landscapes and gardens, was impressed by their work. At first he could not believe that it was the work of such young designers. Pigeat was working in Blois at the time, where the Minister of Culture Jack Lang was mayor. Lang hoped that Pigeat would be able to find young blood to breathe new life into the rather dreary city.

Pigeat launched the duo in Blois. They were immediately given a free hand. Ossart: 'We introduced a new, modern style of vegetation for the whole city. The Loire Valley has a long tradition of parks and gardens, but it was all pretty old-fashioned.' One of their first projects was a roundabout. They planted narrow strips with flowers alternating with types of vegetables in different colours – orange, yellow, grey, purple . . . It was an immediate success.

They did not just modernize the vegetation in Blois; they also carried out 'educational' work among the staff, who were still suspicious of their ideas at first. Sometimes they took the whole group in a bus to go and view gardens elsewhere. It caught on, and although they stopped working for local authorities years ago, their principles are still followed in Blois. After Blois, Maurières and Ossart each went his own way for a couple of years. Ossart went with Pigeat to the large-scale garden exhib-ition in Chaumont-sur-Loire, where he stayed for six or seven years. Maurières set up a school of landscape architecture in Grasse, in the south of France. But they continued to work together on a lot of projects. Eric taught in Arnaud's school and always took part in the annual student excursions.

Ossart: 'Those excursions included Morocco, Egypt and Syria, where we mainly did a lot of land art. For instance, the students were given one day to analyse a landscape, after which they had to draw up a plan to do something with the materials at hand. It was usually in the desert, so there was no question of plants.'

It left them with a permanent love of North Africa. By now they spend a large part of the year in Morocco, where Ossart and Maurières

Eric Ossart, Beauvais, France, 1960
Arnaud Maurières, Montauban, France, 1962
David Gobaut, Soissons, France, 1974
Office in Blois

The
Royal
Mile

have also manifested themselves as architects. They have built their own house there,
followed by designing ten or so homes for
others. 'The Moroccan climate means that you
don't have to distinguish between a house and
a garden. It is a whole, you go through our
garden to get to the kitchen or the dining
room.'
So the oeuvre of Ossart and Maurières is
remarkably wide-ranging. They have designed
various public gardens, including the Jardin
des Paradis in Cordes-sur-Ciel, the Jardin de
l'Alchimiste near Avignon, and the Jardin Noria
in the Gard. Their interest in the history of
cultivated plants is expressed in the public
garden for the Museum Cluny on the Boulevard
Saint-Germain in Paris. For that design they

immersed themselves in the way in which
plants were used medicinally in the Middle
Ages and in their symbolic and religious
connotations. In Cluny they only used plants
that were known in the Middle Ages.
In spite of the diversity, Ossart recognizes
a number of constants in their work: 'Our
gardens are pretty formal in design. They
must not look too natural, we do not make
organic gardens with a lot of curves. The
plants themselves provide enough nature.'
They still travel a lot, recently to Mexico.
'When we come back we are always full of
impressions and ideas, although we will
never make pastiches based on examples
from abroad.
Regarding the design for the Royal Mile,
Ossart says that he conceived of the border
as a long carpet with a regular fabric of
flowers and plants. As the weeks pass,
however, its character will change. 'At first the
border will be regular and regimented. But it
must not be too tidy, so here and there in the
carpet we are putting plants with big flowers
and leaves. They will be small at first, but by
the end of August they will be as much as 2 m
tall. There will be little left of the regular
fabric by then.'
The fact that the Royal Mile border will be
short-lived suits their predilection for
ephemeral gardens. 'Some people like to see
a design that will last for ever, but I think it's
good that it will be replaced by something else
four months later.' Even the houses they build
are in a certain sense ephemeral. The bricks
are made of mud, and if they are not
permanently protected, the walls will collapse
within a couple of years.

Rose garden, Blois, France, autumn 2007

Plant list

Annuals

1. Begonia 'Braveheart'
2. Beta vulgaris (green)
3. Fuchsia magellanica
4. Nicotiana 'Nicki' rose
5. Nicotiana 'Nicki' white
6. Nicotiana sylvestris white
7. Nicotiana x sanderae 'Lime Green'
8. Ricinus communis 'Carmincita' rose
9. Verbena venosa
10. Verbena bonariensis

Bulbs

11. Zantedeschia aethiopica

The
Royal
Mile

The Pink Border

The Royal Mile

Jane Schul

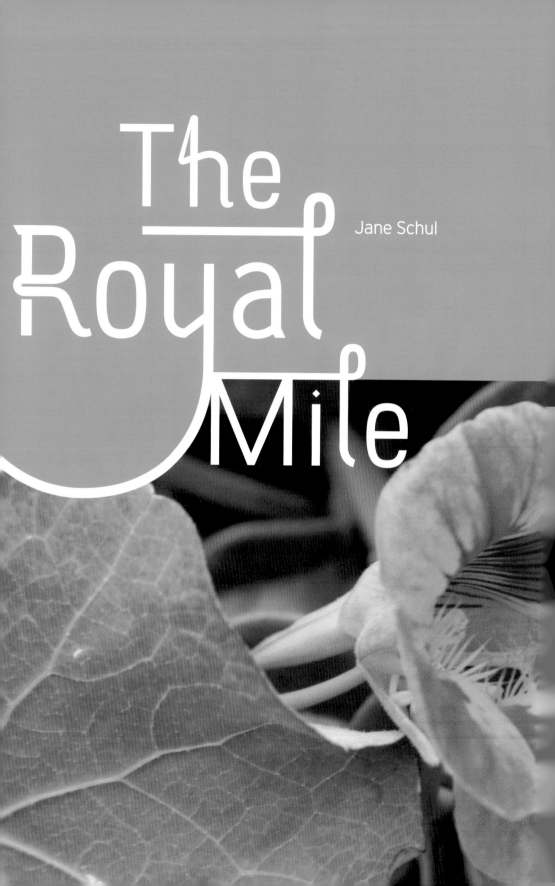

Jacqueline van der Kloet

Ossart & Maurières

Fleur van Zonneveld

Christian Meyer

Christine Orel

Wilko Karmelk

Helen Lewis

Christopher Bradley-Hole

Anita Fischer

Jane Schul

Julie Toll

Ursula Gräfen

The Orange Border

Jane Schul

'The plant world in the moderate climate zone we live in knows an overwhelming supply of blue, white, pink and yellow colours, but very little orange and red ones.

Orange and red are colours belonging to the heat of the tropics and the corresponding bright light. Many of our annual summer plants and bulbs originate from these warm regions, so if we want to make a border here with these orange tints, we have to go on a trip.

A second problem is the fact that many orange flowers belong to the same family, namely those of the composites, which means that each flower is composed of a number of smaller flowers. To prevent the plant scheme from becoming a monoculture by having both the same colour and the same shape, my border and I turned to each of the neighbouring borders for support, the one deep red and the other bright yellow.

In addition we have tried to find flowers with a shape other than the traditional composite and thus we arrived at species like the *Amaranthus*, *Mimulus* and *Tropaeolum*. These are supplemented with a number of blue flowering species for the needed contrast and also to cool down the heat generated by all the other colours.

Finally, to blend the border with the forest background, various ornamental grasses have been added. These go together very well with this tropical mix.' *Jane Schul*

When Jane Schul wants to design and write in peaceful surroundings, she stays in the studio of her country home in Holte, not far from Copenhagen. Our meeting, however, takes place in her office in the middle of a busy district of the Danish capital. 'I come here two or three times a week to elaborate my ideas with my colleagues.'

When she started out for herself more than ten years ago she was still on her own. The first colleague to join her was her son Jonas, who had just graduated from art college and was very interested in gardens and architecture. Now the practice consists of six members and they stopped confining themselves to vegetation designs a long time ago. The firm also covers architecture, urban design and landscape architecture, but those fields are more for the others, such as Jonas. Jane Schul has continued to concentrate on plants.

In Jane Schul's case, the design of vegetation plans is a second career which only began when she was in her late thirties. 'As a child I used to dream of working in gardens. It's a

The Royal Academy for fine Arts, Charlottenborg, Copenhagen, summer 2004

amily addiction.' But, like many other people, he set out initially on a different career. She ecame a weaver. Twenty years later she was ack at school, this time to train as a ndscape architect. 'My specialization was egetation. It was a fairly neglected subject; ndscape architects worked mainly with organic materials. At that time I already nought that it should not be confined to one and concrete, but should include plants o. For me they represented the "softer lues".'

retrospect she does not regard the fference between weaving and working with ants as very big. 'I wanted to become a eaver because I was interested in colours, rms and structures. In my vegetation plans o the same.'

Closer inspection reveals that the city is not such a bad choice for her practice. Many of the commissions are for city gardens and parks. For instance, she recently renovated a series of 20 borders in Tivoli, the amusement park in the heart of Copenhagen. 'Tivoli is open from April to October, so those borders have to look good for six months. I seized the opportunity to show what you can do in a case like that with perennials plus bulbs. The design is based on colour themes with contrasts: a white border with some black flowers, or a yellow border with purple.'

The redesign of a garden behind the sculpture department of the academy of art is well-nigh even more urban. In the nineteenth-century the triangular garden formed part of the Copenhagen botanical gardens. Some of the

The Orange Border   Jane Schul

Framed Growth, Schloss Ippenburg, Bad Essen, Germany, summer 2005

The Royal Danish Garden Societys garden, Frederiksberg, Copenhagen, summer 2006

trees go back to that period, and it is full of blocks of stone that they may want to use for sculptures at some time in the future. Instead of putting all those fragments in a heap, Jane Schul has left them lying scattered through the garden. Some are big enough to sit on. Others function as barriers to guide visitors in the right direction. 'All the same, in choosing the plants we had to bear in mind that the students would occasionally walk right through them. So they have to be able to stand up to that. Moreover, I did not just want the plants to be self-reproducing, but I wanted them to be able to spread. That means plants that are almost weeds. It has turned out to work fantastically.'

The character of the vegetation designs is so dependent on the situation that Jane Schul does not like to refer to a 'signature' of her own. 'I don't think that people will immediately recognize a garden or park as one of my designs. Neither am I out to impose a particular style. I attune my designs to the surroundings, to the available materials, and above all to the people who will use and maintain them.'

For the renovation of a nineteenth-century park in Hillerød, for example, she had to take into account the fact that the expertise and the budget were not what they once were. There was no possibility of restoring the garden to its original, historic state – if only because there were no resources to change the plants each season. And there is no time today for upkeep or to remove the heads after flowering. So Jane Schul chose plants that thrive without much upkeep and whose shape and leaves make them attractive even when

Jane Schul
Frederiksberg, Denmark, 1943
Lives and works in Holte, office in Vanløse
www.schul.dk

The Royal Mile

they are not in flower. 'Colours are always very important – including the colours of the leaf, for when there are no flowers.'

In her opinion, there are plenty of opportunities to introduce seasonal variations without having to keep adding and removing plants all year round. For example, by combining early flowering bulbs with perennials that do not form leaves until late in the year.

Jane Schul drew bright orange for her border on the Royal Mile. 'Plants with orange flowers are often composites that look very much like one another. To prevent my border from becoming an even orange surface, I looked for lots of different shapes. The contrast with the blue flowers brings out the orange even more. In combination with the green of the leaves, the blue also enlivens the border.'

Her Royal Mile border gradually changes character from one end to the other. 'Orange is between yellow and red, so I have added yellow flowers at one end of the border and red ones at the other. The emphasis is fully on orange in the middle. There will not be much in flower soon after the planting in May, but afterwards annuals ought to be able to keep the Royal Mile in flower for its whole duration. And some plants will produce beautiful seed pods after they have flowered.'

Tivoli Gardens, Copenhagen, summer 2006

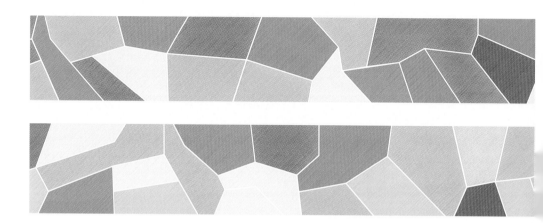

Plant list

Annuals

1. Acorus gramineus 'Ogon'
2. Amaranthus cruentus 'Hot Biscuits'
3. Anagallis monelli 'Skylover Compact'
4. Anchusa azurea 'Dropmore'
5. Angelonia gardneri 'Deep Blue'
6. Asclepias tuberosa 'Orange Shades'
7. Beta vulgaris 'Arancia Leaf Beet'
8. Bupleurum rotundifolium 'Griffiti Green-Yellow'
9. Carthamus tinctorius 'Feuerschopf'
10. Cosmos sulphureus 'Cosmic Red'
11. Cosmos sulphureus 'Diabolo'
12. Gomphrena haageana
13. Helichrysum apiculatum 'Baby Gold'
14. Hordeum jubatum
15. Ipomoea batatas 'Sweetheart Light Green'
16. Ipomoea batatas 'Blacky'
17. Lantana camara 'Prof. Raoux'
18. Mimulus aurantiacus 'Orange'
19. Nicotiana affinis 'Saragota F1 Lime'
20. Nicotiana langsdorffii 'Lime Green'
21. Nigella hispanica
22. Oxalis vulcanicola 'Burgundy'
23. Panicum miliaceum
24. Pennisetum glaucum 'Purple Majesty'
25. Perilla frutescens 'Nankinensis'
26. Rudbeckia hirta 'Autumn Colours'
27. Rudbeckia hirta 'Prairie Sun'
28. Salvia farinacea 'Victoria'
29. Salvia patens
30. Sanvitalia speciosa 'Aztec Gold'
31. Setaria palmifolia
32. Stipa tenuissima
33. Tagetes tenuifolia 'Starfire Mix'
34. Tithonia rotundifolia 'Goldfinger'
35. Tropaeolum majus 'Nanum'

Bulbs

36. Cosmos atrosanguineus
37. Crocosmia 'Emily McKenzie'
38. Crocosmia 'George Davison'
39. Dahlia 'Bantling'
40. Dahlia 'Tam Tam'

38

The Royal Mile

Fleur van Zonneveld

Jacqueline van der Kloet

Ossart & Maurières

Fleur van Zonneveld

Christian Meyer

Christine Orel

Wilko Karmelk

Helen Lewis

Christopher Bradley-Hole

Anita Fischer

Jane Schul

Julie Toll

Ursula Gräfen

The Soft-Orange Border

Fleur van Zonneveld

'Soft-orange summer flowers and bulbs in large quantities together along a sun-shaded avenue in a somewhat rough forest. Such a contrast! This is a big challenge to me as, for most of the time, I look for harmony between plants and their surroundings instead of a distinct contrast. Luckily, soft-orange is one of my favourite colours, especially as it offers so many combination possibilities, both the spectacularly orientated and the quiet harmonious varieties.

The design is aimed at nestling the main colour in between plants that, as far as colour and structure are concerned, offer a change-over to the more natural of the surroundings.

The grasses, crocosmias, digitalises and fennel emphasize this more 'natural' side. They, more or less, will quench the gaudy aspect of the summer flowers.

The border is divided in a shark-tooth pattern with bigger and smaller triangles. In those triangles where the bases face the path, predominantly summer flowers will be planted and in those triangles facing the forest, the 'natural' plants' contribution will increase. The border lines in between the triangles will be accentuated by grasses, resulting in a clear division between the triangles which differ in size, tint and character.

Walking along this border, the almost continuous atmosphere of orange and soft-orange in the foreground will be experienced, changing from solid to soft and back again. Towards the back of the border the plantings will be taller and 'more natural' with grasses, digitalises and fennel.

Along the full length of the border, two festoons of dahlias, crocosmias and gladiolus wind right through the triangles, forming a connecting element, which both softens the orange triangles and lightens up the grassy ones. In this manner, the soft-orange colour, in various shades, is always very much present in this design.' *Fleur van Zonneveld*

It was the *Zeitgeist* of the 1970s that led Fleur van Zonneveld to discover the countryside. 'I was studying in Groningen and it was very popular to live outside the city. We were lucky enough to be able to rent an enormous farm for 100 guilders a month in 1972. It had a beautiful romantic garden and no less than 100 standard fruit trees.'

She soon discovered that gardening was in her blood. It was strongly encouraged by Rob

Top: Border, De Kleine Plantage, Eenrum, the Netherlands, September 2006

Bottom: Border, De Kleine Plantage, Eenrum, the Netherlands, June 2006

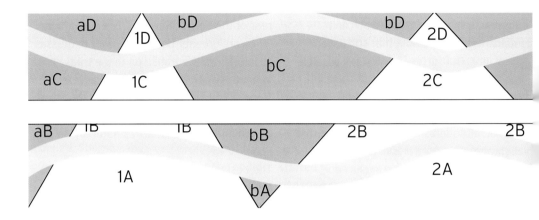

The Soft-Orange Border

Plant list

Annuals

1. Abutilon malvacea 'Salmon'
2. Agastache 'Apricot Sprite'
3. Anthirrhinum majus 'Bronze Rocket'
4. Asclepias curassavica 'Red Butterfly'
5. Begonia 'Champagne'
6. Begonia 'Illumination Apricot'
7. Begonia 'Richard Galle'
8. Calibrachoa 'Crackling Fire'
9. Calibrachoa 'Golden Terracotta'
10. Calibrachoa 'Orange Glow
11. Carex buchananii 'Red Rooster'
12. Diascia 'Bleek Oranje'
13. Diascia 'Tangerine'
14. Digitalis 'Carillon'
15. Digitalis 'Sutton's Apricot'
16. Foeniculum vulgare 'Giant Bronze'
17. Helichrysum petiolare 'Silver'
18. Hordeum jubatum
19. Impatiens 'Seashell Apricot'
20. Lantana 'Lucky Peach'
21. Lantana 'Orange King'
22. Mimulus aurantiacus 'Orange'
23. Oxalis vulcanicola 'Dark Form'
24. Pennisetum glaucum 'Purple Majesté'
25. Pennisetum setaceum
26. Pennisetum setaceum 'Rubrum'
27. Pennisetum setaceum 'Rubrum Compactum'
28. Pennisetum villosum
29. Phygelius 'Candy Drop Salmon Orange'
30. Tagetes patula 'Linnaeus'
31. Tropaeolum 'Salmon Glow'
32. Tropaeolum 'Tip Top Apricot'
33. Verbena 'Peaches and Cream'

Bulbs

34. Crocosmia 'Constance'
35. Crocosmia 'Columbus'
36. Crocosmia 'Voyager'
37. Crocosmia masonorum
38. Dahlia 'David Howard'
39. Dahlia 'H.S. First Love'
40. Dahlia 'Moonfire'
41. Dahlia 'Classic Elise'
42. Gladiolus 'Maxima'
43. Gladiolus 'Sunglow'

The Soft-Orange Border

The Royal Mile

Julie Toll

Wilko Karmelk

Helen Lewis

Jacqueline van der Kloet

Christopher
Bradley-Hole

Anita Fischer

Ossart & Maurières

Jane Schul

Fleur van Zonneveld

Julie Toll

Christian Meyer

Ursula Gräfen

Christine Orel

The Yellow Border

Julie Toll

'Like a beam of sunlight, these yellow flowers happily stand out against the backdrop of the waving grasses and the warmer tones of the orange and copper flowers.
The random combinations of these plants are reminiscent of a wild summer cornfield where nature has gently shaped the planting design. Bold clumps of *Helianthus*, the double flowers of the *Centaurea* and the drumheads of the *Craspedia* punctuate this otherwise soft planting and remind us that the hand of man is never far away.' *Julie Toll*

Julie Toll lives and works in Hertfordshire, some 50 km north of London. Her assignments vary from small city gardens to estates – not only in the UK, but also in Ireland and on the continent. On top of that she flies two or three times a year to the island of Nevis in the Caribbean to design gardens for a constantly growing group of clients there. 'One of my clients went to the island for a holiday some years ago. When he came back he told me that he would like to buy a plot of land on it. He said: "I want to build a house, but only if you agree to design the garden."

That's how it all started. I would love to have a house on Nevis as well, but I'm always so busy when I'm there that I've never had the time to look for anything.'
Julie Toll had already acquired experience with tropical plants years earlier when she was director of an interior landscape company. At that time she already knew a hundred or so types of tropical plants. In the meantime her repertoire has widened dramatically and she now uses between 200 and 300 different sorts. 'The beauty of Nevis is that they're in their natural setting.'
Although she does not consider designing a garden on Nevis to be essentially different from designing a garden in England, there are of course big differences in the climate and the range of plants. Things never stand still there. Not just plants, but also pests and diseases multiply very quickly in that tropical climate, and the seasons are less extreme. There are no experienced landscape contractors on the island either. In other respects, however, she says that she is the same garden designer all over the world.

Private garden, Hertfordshire, England, July 2007

The Yellow Border

Julie Toll

Private garden, Hertfordshire, England, July 2007

Julie Toll has lived among plants since she was a girl. She was born on a fruit and vegetable farm and was growing and selling her own tomatoes by the time she was 13. Later she went to horticultural college for four years to study the growing and production of trees and shrubs. It was a practical course which paid hardly any attention to garden design. All the same, that thorough knowledge of plants, soil science and botany was to stand her in good stead later. The students had to identify 50 new plants a week. It was only years later, after she had decided to set up her own practice, that Julie Toll attended a specialized design

course in the English Garden School in Chelsea.

To attract clients she had to find a way of publicizing her new firm, so in 1990 she decided to try to get into the prestigious Chelsea Flower Show, the biggest annual garden show in England. Julie Toll approached John Chambers, a wild flower seed specialist, and proposed that she design a wild flower garden for him to sponsor at the next Chelsea flower show. John Chambers was happy to promote the sale of his seeds. 'So I was the first ever to present a real garden with wild plants in the show. Until then the Royal Horticultural Society, which organizes

Chelsea, had always regarded wild plants as weeds. The public loved it and I won my first gold medal.'

Julie Toll has often designed gardens for the Chelsea Flower Show since then, each time characterized by the choice of wild and endemic plants – but as part of a much wider range. She has won a total of seven gold medals.

The reputation that she acquired at Chelsea prompted the BBC to invite her to present the very popular television programme *Gardens by Design*. In the course of the series of six programmes, she showed how she designed a garden step by step for a family. It started with discussing the brief with the family, followed by the design and its implementation. 'It was a great success. It was the first garden design programme on British TV. It's been followed by many more since.'

Julie Toll says that others describe her work as 'contemporary natural'. 'I like my garden designs to look natural. I'm also fond of using natural materials such as natural stone and rocks. The contemporary look comes from the fact that I work with strong structures. These are formed by elements such as trees, hedges, paths, walls, or other hard landscape features. I prefer not to make those structures square or rectangular. If a garden lends itself to it, I prefer flowing shapes with a lot of movement. It's the plants that add softness to those structures, and I mix the types of plants as much as I can. I never limit myself to one sort.' She mostly designs private gardens: city or country gardens, she has no preference. Big and small gardens both have their specific complications and she enjoys those

differences. 'In a small garden you can often design it all in one go and then it's finished. Whereas you design a big garden gradually, making use of the existing features.'

Julie Toll designed a border (colour: yellow) for the Royal Mile which evokes the atmosphere of a meadow with wild plants. All of the plants are cultivated, but they give the impression of being wild. She uses a lot of grasses and plants annuals in between them. For the structure, but also for what she calls 'a bit of madness', she has chosen big sunflowers. 'They are almost like people walking through the meadow. I haven't introduced any other shapes or patterns into the border. It's what I call a matrix of plants, with everything mixed together. It is all one, punctuated by those big, mad sunflowers.'

Meadow of wild plants, Hertfordshire, England, June 2005

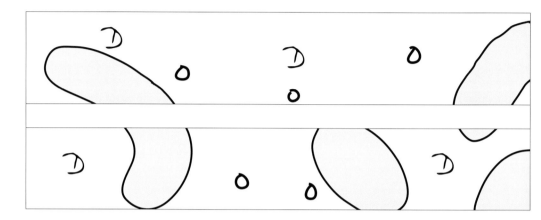

Plant list

Annuals

1. Craspedia globosa 'Drumstick'
2. Verbascum hybridum 'Cotswold Queen'
3. Agastache 'Apricot Spire'
4. Centaurea moschata 'Dairy Maid'
5. Bidens ferulifolia 'Golden Goddess'
6. Rudbeckia hirta 'Marmalade'
7. Rudbeckia hirta 'Irish Eyes'
8. Scabiosa atropurpurea 'Chat Noir'
9. Coreopsis basalis 'Gold King'
10. Leonitis 'Staircase'
11. Helianthus 'Moonshine'
12. Briza maxima
13. Melica transsilvanica 'Red Spire'
14. Pennisetum ruppelianum
15. Hordeum vulgare distichum

Bulbs

16. Dahlia 'Honka'
17. Crocosmia 'Angel Wings'

16

The Yellow Border

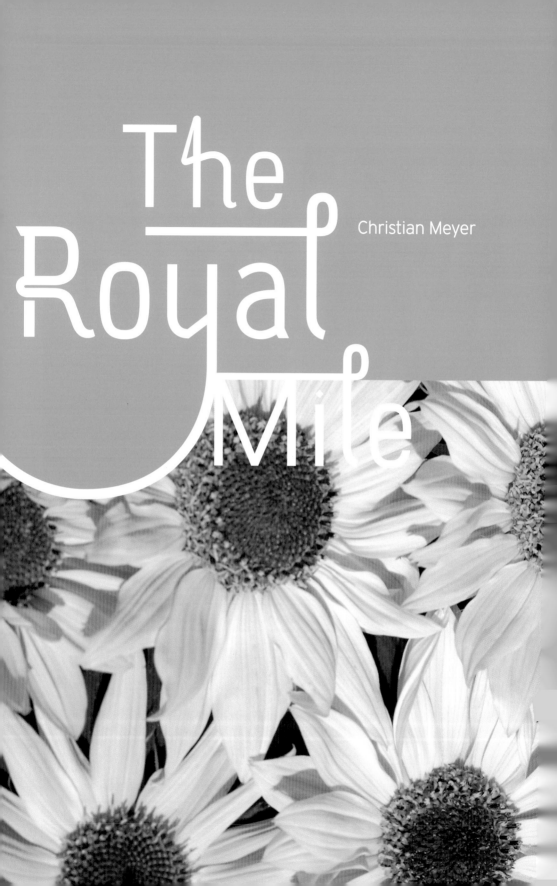

The Royal Mile

Christian Meyer

Jacqueline van der Kloet

Ossart & Maurières

Fleur van Zonneveld

Christian Meyer

Christine Orel

Wilko Karmelk

Helen Lewis

Christopher
Bradley-Hole

Anita Fischer

Jane Schul

Julie Toll

Ursula Gräfen

'Where flower borders are concerned, a soft-yellow has belonged to my favourites for many years now. Even in very hot weather, the soft-yellow colour always keeps a cool and refreshing promise. In addition, it is an excellent colour to combine with bright yellow, which seems warmer but is at the same time very often less elegant and a bit too pushy.

The composition of a soft-yellow border is the most successful when various shades of yellow, such as sulphur, lime and corn but also green-yellow and crème-yellow are combined in the right quantities. Numerous green-yellow leaves of perennials are a great help to keep the colour effect for a longer period of time.

To achieve the most natural looking result, a combination of various growth patterns was looked for: both plants with a climbing, loose growth pattern and plants with a more compact or even crawling growth pattern are part of the whole, which here and there is broken up by solitary plants.

The total length of 70 m has been divided into seven parts which alternate in irregular fashion. Together, however, they form one harmonious entity. Because of this the border is enchanting from beginning to end.' *Christian Meyer*

By the middle of the 1990s Christian Meyer thought it was time for something else. He had been working mainly on vegetation plans for various districts of Berlin and he felt that the time had come to use his design talent for private clients. As far as private gardens were concerned, however, Meyer regarded Berlin then and now as 'a developing country'. The few private projects on which he had already worked had been disappointing. The clients did not want to invest much in them and turned out not to be very interested in his ideas. Meyer saw the way out of the impasse in a leap forwards. He took the initiative himself. 'It's difficult to convey what you want do to with words alone, you need a real garden. So I thought: I have to create a model garden in the middle of the city.' After looking around, Meyer found a small triangular plot beside the Kurfürstendamm. He asked the Charlottenbur

ty garden, Kurfürstendamm, Berlin-Charlottenburg, Germany, May 2007

strict council to let him create a garden
ere on his own initiative. It took two years
r the permit to come through, on condition
at it would not cost the district anything.
rtunately, two well-known nurseries were
epared to sponsor him and to supply the
ants free of charge. Maintenance was his
sponsibility; he brought in students from the
stitute where he was teaching at the time.
itially only few people with garden interests
oticed Meyer's city garden at the busy
ossroads. 'But when I started writing about
I suddenly made a name for myself with all
e landscape architects in the Federal
epublic. Everyone who read garden
agazines had suddenly heard about the
urfürstendamm project, so I was invited to
mposia and congresses to report on the
xperience of gardening on an inner city
affic island.' Meanwhile the garden became

well-known with the ordinary people of Berlin
as well, was awarded several distinctions, and
celebrated its tenth anniversary in April 2008.
This did not lead to a spate of private garden
designs, however. Meyer's commissions came
from other quarters. He was asked for plans
for the courtyards enclosed by apartment
blocks that are so typical of Berlin, or for front
gardens facing the street. But most of the
work that has come to him since then is from
garden architects who know less about plants
than he does, who have asked him for
vegetation designs. Sometimes public clients
insist on his drawing up the vegetation plan.
'Established garden designers don't like that,
they think that they can take it in their stride.
Younger garden architects are more open,
they're not ashamed to come to me.'
Christine Orel, one of the designers on the
Royal Mile, was one of those who contacted

The Soft-Yellow Border

Rose garden in Tiergarten Park, Berlin, Germany, July 2006

Spreebogen Park, Berlin, Germany, May 2007

everything, really everything was laid down in advance. Three years later I had finished and decided to continue my studies at the university, where there was much more freedom.'

To fund his university studies, Meyer started looking for work. 'I had the good fortune that the 1985 'Bundesgartenschau' was to be held in Berlin, and I found a job there as a student. I worked mainly in the perennial garden. After the 'Bundesgartenschau' I was given a further two-year contract to help to create a permanent design for the park. Until then I'd never really known what I wanted to do with my training, but at that time working with plants made me really keen on perennial planting designs.'

Meyer's first real commission came in 1988: a vegetation plan beneath the old trees of a boulevard in the Spandau district. One thing led to another. Until 1998 he worked on public vegetation plans in various districts of the city. He did not confine himself to the design, but also instructed the staff on maintenance. He sometimes supervised and documented the projects for years.

At first Christian Meyer worked mainly with perennials. 'But I've also learnt a lot about annuals through working together with Christine. I would like to work with them more often, that's why the Royal Mile in Apeldoorn appeals so much to me.'

No plant is taboo for Meyer. Not even the conifer that is looked down on by most garden designers. 'A plant is never itself responsible for being used in a boring way. Conifers – like most people, I never found them very interesting. But my ideas changed after the

Christian Meyer. She was looking for someone to help her to design the perennials at the 2001 'Bundesgartenschau' in Potsdam, just outside Berlin, and she needed a perennials specialist. Later they also worked together on the 'Internationale Gartenschau' in Rostock in 2003 and a 'Landesgartenschau' in Brandenburg.

Meyer moved from the Ruhr region to Berlin at the age of 19 to study landscape architecture in Berlin. 'A rigid course in which

Christian Meyer
Bochum, Germany, 1959
Lives and works in Berlin
www.buero-christian-meyer.de

The
Royal
Mile

fall of the Wall. I suddenly saw conifers in the gardens in Potsdam, which was in the former GDR, that had been there for long years and looked like sculptures. They formed splendid contrasts with the autumnal colours of the perennials. So I discovered how valuable they can be and now use them myself occasionally.' Meyer's border for the Royal Mile is divided into seven sections. Two modules, each with its own combination of plants, alternate: four times module A and three times module B. Three main features are prominent through-out the entire border as a constant factor: dahlias, large nicotine plants, and soft-yellow sunflowers. He has also used large groups of

mixed plants to give the border the character of a meadow. 'They are not really meadow plants, but plants from the farmhouse garden, such as snapdragons and Chinese asters. There will be plants accentuating the colour – my colour is soft-yellow – with their foliage, such as a sweet potato with a yellow leaf. Finally I have chosen a few plants to fill the border during the first few weeks until the other plants take over.' Christian Meyer found it difficult to limit himself. 'There are so many beautiful annual flowers. There are countless lovely yellow variants of the Chinese asters alone, with very differently shaped flowers. But I could only choose two.'

Karl Foerster Garden in the Britzer Garten, Berlin-Neuköln, Germany, June 2006

Plant list

Annuals

1. Acorus 'Ogon'
2. Agastache 'Blue Fortune'
3. Agastache 'Green White'
4. Ageratum houstonianum 'Weißer Schnitt'
5. Amaranthus caudatus 'Grünschwanz'
6. Ammi majus
7. Anthirrhinum majus 'Rocket White'
8. Anthirrhinum majus 'Rocket Yellow'
9. Callistephus chinensis 'Benary's Princess Yellow'
10. Callistephus chinensis 'Kompliment Yellow'
11. Cleome spinosa 'Helen Campbell'
12. Coleus blumei 'Nevada'
13. Coleus blumei 'Wizzard Jade'
14. Cosmos bipinnatus 'Sonata White'
15. Euphorbia marginata 'Icicle'
16. Helianthus debilis 'Italian White'
17. Helichrysum petiolare 'Gold'
18. Ipomoea batatas 'Marguerite'
19. Lamium maculatum 'Anne Greenaway'
20. Lantana camara 'Luxor Creme White'
21. Molucella laevis 'Bells of Ireland'
22. Nicotiana alata 'Saratoga Lime'
23. Nicotiana langsdorffii
24. Nicotiana sylvestris
25. Ocimum hybride 'Magic Blue'
26. Rudbeckia hirta 'Prairie Sun'
27. Salvia farinacea 'Strata'
28. Tagetes erecta nana 'Vanilla'
29. Tagetes erecta plena 'Zitronenprinz'
30. Tagetes patula nana 'Yellow Hero'
31. Verbena bonariensis
32. Zinnia elegans 'Benarys Riesen Violett'
33. Zinnia elegans 'Dahlienblütige Riesenlimette'
34. Zinnia elegans 'Oklahoma White'
35. Zinnia Hybrids 'Profusion White'

Bulbs

36. Dahlia 'Glorie van Heemstede'
37. Galtonia candicans
38. Lilium tigrinum 'Citronella'

37

The Soft-Yellow Border

Christian Meyer

36

38

Jacqueline van der Kloet	Ossart & Maurières	Fleur van Zonneveld	Christian Meyer	Christine Orel
Wilko Karmelk / Helen Lewis	Christopher Bradley-Hole / Anita Fischer	Jane Schul	Julie Toll	Ursula Gräfen

The White Border

Ursula Gräfen

'White is the lightest colour of all. White is the colour of snow and ice. White is white, as the sunlight is almost completely reflected.

A border of just white tints looks distinctive, but also aloof and cool.

Here, however, white gets a different character as it is combined with the warm colours of the sun, the blue of the sky and the always present green of the foliage. The distinctiveness and aloofness gives way to a flamboyant jollity. This is mainly because many varieties of loosely floating flowering patterns were selected, in addition to cheery, colourful tints. They dance in the wind and accentuate the airiness of the border.' *Ursula Gräfen*

Ursula Gräfen's love of plants was kindled at an early age. Her father, a garden architect who himself came from a gardening family, played an important role in that. He was very interested in native wild plants and was only too keen to pass his knowledge on to his children.

All the same, it was not until just before her final exams at school that she decided to train as a landscape architect at the Weihenstephan institute in Friesing. By now she has been working as a landscape architect for almost 30 years. After gaining experience in every aspect of design with two firms, she started up her own practice in Munich in 1999.

Her enthusiasm for working with plants has only increased over the years. She became particularly keen on planting designs. 'Many of the commissions that I am offered are entirely planting assignments. They are often private gardens, but may also be exhibitions, or large projects such as a Sinnesgarten (a garden of the senses) or the clematises in the gardens of Castle Trauttmansdorff in Merano.' It is above all the changing lifecycle of plants that appeals to her. 'That is what distinguishes plants from all other design resources. Because they are living materials, the time factor plays a decisive role. Plantings continue to evolve, and are constantly changing as a result. You can't put those changes down on paper, but you have to bear them in mind all the time when you are making a design.'

If the plantings are to be at their best, the setting in which they are placed must also be right. In that case a contrast can be created between the luxuriance of the plants and the geometric grid of paths, walls, and perhaps well-trimmed hedges. Still, such a grid must remain in the background – after all, it is the

Rose garden Schloss Ippenburg, Bad Essen, Germany, summer 2005

The White Border

Ursula Gräfen

plants that should be in the limelight. Does she have favourite plants? 'No, I don't have any particular favourites. Of course, I use some plants more than others, for example because they are so uncomplicated, or because they add something special to the garden throughout the year – first with the flowers, then with the fruits, and finally with the autumn colours. Examples are the snowy mespilus and the ornamental apple. I also often choose perennials that flower late in the year; they look nice throughout the season too. But there is such an enormous variety of fascinating plants that I do not want to get pinned down to a limited number of favourites.'

There are some plants that she has grown to appreciate in the course of time. At first she was not very enthusiastic about roses, for instance, but when she was working on a design for the Landesgartenschau in Ingolstadt in 1992, she suddenly developed a passion for roses. 'We had included a rose garden in our competition entry. Still, in no way did I want the dominant monoculture that you so often see – with colour combinations of blood red with pink and yellow and hardly any leaves left once the summer has started. Luckily for us, that was the time when the so-called English rose was introduced in Germany, with full blossoms in the style of historical roses, in the most beautiful pastel tints – and almost all with a seductive scent. With roses like that I was suddenly able to imagine what our rose garden ought to look like.'

She did not stop at that one rose garden. She has designed a good many of them since then,

Private garden, Munich, Germany, summer 2007

Ursula Gräfen
Cologne, Germany, 1955
Lives and works in Munich

The Royal Mile

often combined with perennials. Perennials not only prolong the period in which there are flowering plants in a garden, but they also offer the opportunity to add extra accents with more colours and shapes.

The basic colour of her Royal Mile border is white, 'the sum of all colours'. According to Ursula Gräfen, white can be applied in various ways. You can choose to make white the only colour. The border will then look distinguished, but also cool and aloof. After all, white is the colour of ice and snow.

A border like that would be out of place on the Royal Mile. A distinguished border does not fit in with the natural surroundings of the wood and the meadow-like character of the Royal Mile. That is why she has opted for an alternative approach. 'I have combined white with warm, sunny tints, such as yellow and orange, and blue, the colour of the sky. Combinations like that instantly change the character of the white: no longer noble and distinguished, but airy and cheerful.'

Not just the colours but also the shape of the plants selected bring about that lightness of touch. Flowers on taller stalks pop up here and there, waving gently in the breeze. The border is composed on the basis of two modules with different combinations of plants, but with the same character. As a great diversity with many contrasts may already be expected on the Royal Mile, Ursula Gräfen has conceived of the two modules not as opposites, but as variations on the same theme. The mood is thus the same everywhere: not a tightly organized, dense border, but a variety of plants that give the impression of being loosely interwoven.

Pot garden, office Ursula Gräfen, Munich, Germany, summer 2007

Garden of the Town Hall, Landsberg am Lech, Germany, summer 2006

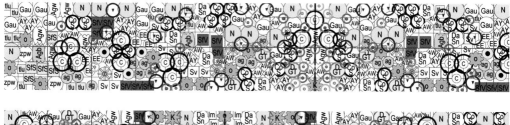

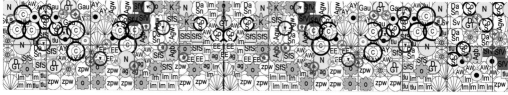

Plant list

Annuals

1. Agastache mexicana 'Green White'
2. Agastache 'Blue Fortune'
3. Ageratum houstonianum 'Blue Horizon' F1
4. Antirrhinum 'Rocket Yellow' F1
5. Antirrhinum majus 'Rocket White' F1
6. Antirrhinum majus 'Rocket Bronze' F1
7. Chrysanthemum (Tanacetum) parthenium 'Gold Moon'
8. Cleome spinosa 'Helen Campbell'
9. Cleome 'Sparkler White' F1
10. Cosmos bipinnatus 'Sonata White'
11. Cosmos sulphureus 'Sunset'
12. Cosmos sulphureus 'Diablo'
13. Euphorbia marginata 'Icicle'
14. Gaura lindheimeri 'Whirling Butterflies'
15. Lobularia maritima 'Snow Chrystals'
16. Melampodium paludosum 'Derby'
17. Nicotiana langsdorffii
18. Pennisetum villosum
19. Rudbeckia hirta 'Prairie Sun'
20. Salvia farinacea 'Victoria'
21. Salvia farinacea 'Silber'
22. Salvia viridis 'White Swan'
23. Scabiosa atropurpurea 'Oxford Blue'
24. Tagetes erecta 'Gold Coins Sovereign'
25. Tagetes tenuifolia 'Lulu'
26. Tanacetum parthenium 'Tetraweiss'
27. Verbena bonariensis
28. Zinnia hybrida 'Profusion White'

Bulbs

29. Dahlia (bal) 'Golden Torch'
30. Dahlia (decoratieve) 'Sneeuwstorm'
31. Dahlia (decoratieve) 'Oranje Nassau'
32. Dahlia (decoratieve) 'Kelly'
33. Liatris 'Floristan Alba'

5

30

The White Border

Ursula Gräfen

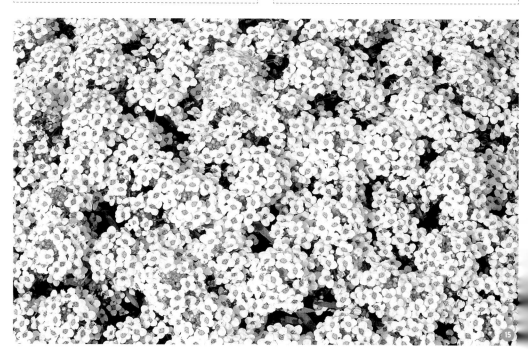

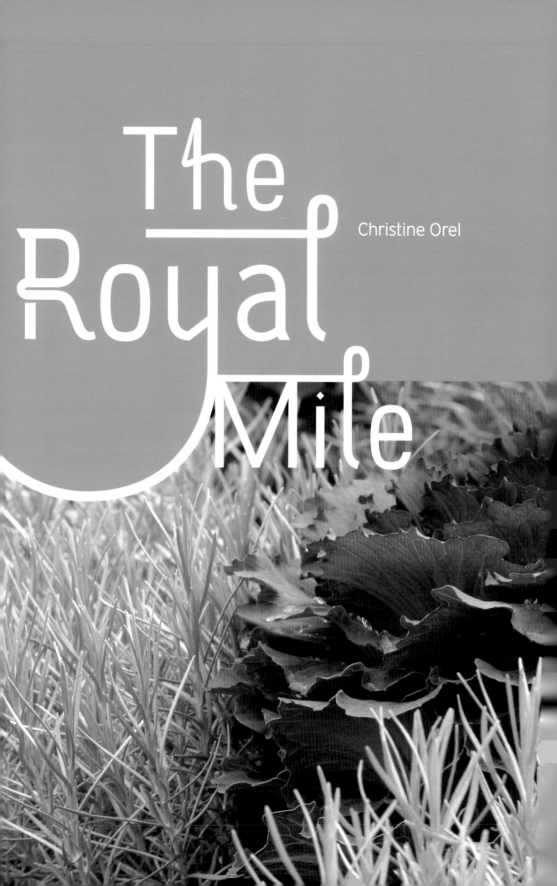

The
Royal
Mile

Christine Orel

Jacqueline van der Kloet

Ossart & Maurières

Fleur van Zonneveld

Christian Meyer

Christine Orel

Wilko Karmelk

Helen Lewis

Christopher Bradley-Hole

Anita Fischer

Jane Schul

Julie Toll

Ursula Gräfen

The Greyish-Green Border Christine Orel

'Can grey and green, in fact, be called colours in the garden world? Anyone who is looking for distinctive inflorescences in yellow and red or for tall, spicated shapes in rose and violet will not find them in the greyish-green border.

It is possible to make plant combinations with grey and green which are as attractive and versatile as working with more pronounced colours; the rules are just different.

The shape of the leaf and the appearance of the plant is in this case much more important than the colours of the flowers. By alternating large-leaved plants such as the sweet potato (*Ipomoea batatas 'Marguerite'*) with the *Helichrysum stoechas 'Icicles'*, fascinating contrasts will develop, which will please spectators. Also the fireweed (*Kochia scoparia*) with leaves that are almost needle-like, in combination with the round-leaved *Eucalyptus 'Silver Dollar'* guarantees an exciting combination.

Still, in all these greys and greens a light colour accent, such as lavender blue, lemon yellow or salmon rose, should be present. Mixed plant groups will be alternated with groups of one species, making sure that the highs of the plants increase towards the back of the border. There, room will be made for stately plants such as flowering tobacco (*Nicotiana sylvestris 'Only the Lonely'*) or Mexican hyssop (*Agastache mexicana 'Green White'*).

In this border the planting is shaped in a manner which is in between classical and a wildflower meadow.' *Christine Orel*

Christine Orel's designs usually have more in mind than just a beautiful garden. If the opportunity arises, she wants them to tell a story as well. 'I once designed a garden that referred to the cleansing of the ground that had been carried out shortly before. I wanted the plants to show that there had been something very ugly in the ground, so they were unusual and not particularly cheerful but aggressive. Among those I included were black cabbage, copper-coloured snapdragon, black dahlias, black grasses, and plants with grey leaves.'

'Opinions are sharply divided on designs like that. People either like them or hate them. I like to provoke that debate. But I also make beautiful, romantic and sweet gardens. It all

Top: Border design, Steiermark, Austria, 2005
Bottom: Border design, Kronach, Germany, 2002

The Greyish-Green Border | Christine Orel

Border design, Wies, Steiermark, Austria, 2005

depends on the history and atmosphere of the spot. I like to express that in the garden design.'

Christine Orel had to come a long way before she dared to create a garden on the theme of polluted soil. 'I wouldn't have been able to do it at the start, but I soon discovered that I needed to use the plants for a theme, that I shouldn't confine myself to combining red fields next to yellow ones. So I started to design an impressionist garden, or a cheerful garden, or a heliogarden with plants that referred to the sun.'

Initially she had planned to embark on a musical career, but she was not good enough to become a soloist and music teachers were almost all without a job at the time. Her father, an architect, suggested that she follow in his footsteps, but she considered that

profession too static. She preferred plants because you never know how they are going to develop. You always have to meekly wait and see what happens. So Christine Orel went to study landscape architecture at the Fachhochschule Weihenstephan in Freising, where Ursula Gräfen and Anita Fischer also studied.

'Plants were already my favourite subject; we had a very good tutor. But you still have to keep developing afterwards; plants are about constant learning and experimenting. A good knowledge of plants calls for such intense involvement that few designers concentrate entirely on them. I don't think there are more than 10 or 15 in the whole of Germany.'

So vegetation is Orel's speciality. Her firm does everything in the garden, including moving soil, walls and benches. But if she is asked to design a park, it is usually specially for the vegetation. Sometimes a client asks the designer to leave the plants entirely up to her. Often it is the designer himself who brings her in. Christine Orel would actually like to design a whole park for once, but the firm has not yet received a commission of that kind. 'Apparently, we have the reputation of being vegetation designers who specialize in annual summer flowers, while I'm just as keen on perennials.'

Before designing a garden, Christine Orel first takes a look at the house and its occupants. 'I always try to find out what kind of a style people have around them. The views of the surrounding landscape are also very important. Visual axes make the space much larger than just the garden.'

So the choice of plants will depend mainly on

Christine Orel
Reutlingen, Germany, 1962
Lives and works in Aurachtal
www.OrelPlusTeam.de

The Royal Mile

the situation. All the same, she has her favourites, such as the Kolkwitzia, or Beautybush: 'An extremely romantic plant that can grow up to 3 m high and has thousands of hanging pink blossoms in May and June. But it only works in a romantic setting, I wouldn't use it for a provocative garden.' Materials have to match the mood of the site too: 'I can't say that I only like concrete or steel. Sometimes I apply used materials. I once designed a plastic bench that looked like an amoeba. Of course, the intention was to provoke, too.'

She says that she always provides contrasts. For example, in a setting with a historic atmosphere she will work with strong forms and elements, while allowing the vegetation a large measure of freedom. 'My gardens always have spots where hard and soft meet.' Christine Orel had initially picked the straw with the colour pink for the Royal Mile. She liked the colour, but it was too dull for her. Eric Ossart and Ursula Gräfen were not content with their colours either: white and grey-green. 'We swapped our colours so that everyone was happy. Eric got pink, Ursula white, and I greyish-green. Greyish-green is a difficult colour, especially because my border is in a shady spot. Plants that grow in the shade are almost never grey. But I found it exciting to work on the basis of a colour that was not really associated with flowers.' She designed the Royal Mile border following a basic module with variations. Certain elements recur without the border becoming monotonous. The basis module itself already has a rhythm with an alternation of plants that grow upwards or sideways. If all goes as

planned, there will be flowers throughout the period. The salmon-coloured sage and the snapdragons will flower early; if the heads are removed after flowering, they may blossom again. Ay any rate the dahlias will flower last. The greyish-green colour will have to come mainly from the leaves, as she does not think that there are many plants with green-grey flowers. Leaf colours are important for Christine Orel anyway, and so is the reciprocal interaction of their forms.

Still, her borders have to be attractive even without colours. She has a simple but effective test for that: 'A black-and-white photo is the best conceivable check. Only then can you see whether the arrangement and the rhythm are right. They sometimes say: "Christine Orel, isn't that the woman with those funny colours, who places orange next to pink?" But I always position them so that the border also looks good in black-and-white.'

Border design, Kronach, Germany, 2002

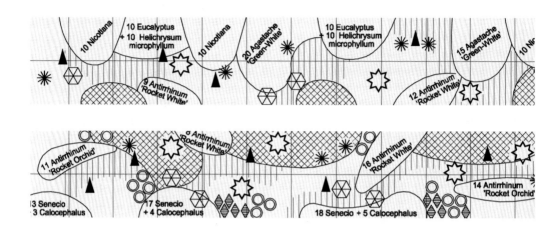

Plant list

Annuals

1. Agastache mexicana 'Green White'
2. Ammi majus 'White Green'
3. Antirrhinum majus F1 'Rocket Orchid'
4. Antirrhinum majus F1 'Rocket White'
5. Begonia x tuberhybrida 'Champagne'
6. Brassica oleracea conv. 'Nero di Toscana'
7. Callistephus chinensis 'Hulk'
8. Calocephalus brownii
9. Centaurea 'Alpine Blue'
10. Cleome spinosa 'Helen Campbell'
11. Eucalyptus 'Silverdollar'
12. Gaura lindheimeri 'Whirling Butterflies'
13. Helichrysum stoechas 'Icicles'
14. Helichrysum microphylla 'Silver'
15. Ipomoea batatas 'Marguerite'
16. Kochia scoparia 'Trichophylla'
17. Lamium maculatum 'White Nancy'
18. Lobelia x speciosa F1 'Fan Lachsrosa'

19. Lotus berthelotii 'Orange'
20. Molucella laevis 'Bells of Ireland'
21. Nicotiana speciosa 'Green Bells'
22. Nicotiana sylvestris 'Only the Lonely'
23. Pennisetum setaceum 'Rubrum'
24. Phygelius 'Candydrop Cream'
25. Pilea microphylla
26. Salvia farinacea 'Silver'
27. Salvia officinalis 'Icterina'
28. Senecio cineraria 'Cirrus'
29. Verbena bonariensis
30. Zinnia elegans 'Envy Selektion S&G'
31. Zinnia elegans 'Oklahoma Lachs'

Bulbs

32. Dahlia 'Chat Noir'
33. Dahlia 'Yvonne'
34. Tulbaghia violacea

20

The Greyish-Green Border

Christine Orel

The Greyish-Green Border | Christine Orel

Colophon

This book was published on the occasion of the Apeldoorn International Triennial from 11 June till 28 September 2008.

Triënnale Apeldoorn

The Royal Mile was sponsored by

Centraal beheer achmea

We extend our gratitude to
- International Flower Bulb Centre (www.bloembollen-centrum.nl)
- Kwekerij Davelaar, Woudenberg (www.crocosmia.nl)
- Kwekerij Overaa, Breda
- Kwekerij Rijnbeek en Zoon B.V. , Boskoop (www.Rijnbeek.com)

Concept and organisation: Jacqueline van der Kloet
Production: Gemeente Apeldoorn, Apeldoorn

Publication
Authors: Jacqueline van der Kloet, Olof Koekebakker
(all interviews with the designers)
Translations: Peter Mason
Text editing: D'Laine Camp
Design: Michelangela, Utrecht
Lithography and printing: Drukkerij Die Keure, Bruges
Paper: Satimat 135 grs
Project coordination: Barbera van Kooij, NAi Publishers
Publisher: NAi Publishers, Rotterdam

Photo credits

- Ernst Benary Samenzucht GmbH p. 83[27], 104[6], 106[13], 107[12], 116[9][21], 119[10], 128[24], 131[13][19]
- Bulb'Argence p. 39
- Chiltern Seeds p. 102, 104[7], 105[11], 106[14], 107[10]
- Christopher Bradley-Hole p. 47
- Collectie Apeldoorn p. 9
- De Kleine Plantage p. 84, 87, 91, 92[30][9], 93[24][22], 94
- Ferdinandushof p. 23, 24, 25, 26, 27, 28[19][1], 29, 30[5], 31[35]
- Anita Fischer p. 51
- Florensis p. 40[8][3][2], 41[4], 42, 43[7]
- Forschungsanstalt für Gartenbau Weihenstephan p. 116[8], 127, 128[28], 130[8], 129[6]
- Goldsmith Seeds p. 41[1]
- Ursula Gräfen p. 123-126
- Harptree Nursery p. 43[12]
- Van Hemert Seeds p. 44, 119[23]
- K. Sahin Zaden B.V. p. 30[14], 31[38], 108
- S&G Flowers/ Syngenta Seeds p. 31[27], 38, 40[2], 68, 83[29]
- Kiepenkerl/Nebelung Plant-Breeding p. 80[10], 83[2], 92[7], 128[10]
- Jacqueline van der Kloet p. 11, 15, 35, 36, 37
- Maarten Laupman p. 8, 17, 22, 34, 74, 86, 98, 110, 122, 134
- Andrew Lawson p. 46 top
- Marianne Majerus Garden Images p. 99-101
- Christian Meyer p. 111-113
- Christine Orel p. 132, 135-143
- Ossart & Maurières p. 60-66, p. 70[2][11]
- Hugh Palmer p. 47 bottom
- PanAmerican Seed Europe BV, p. 59[12], 119[28]
- Rijnbeek & Zoon B.V., Vaste Planten p. 13
- Jane Schul p. 72, 75-77, 80[6], 82
- Thompson & Morgan p. 55, 56, 57, 58, 59[2], 96, 104[3], 105[5]
- Visions Pictures p. 16, 20, 28[45], 32, 40[11], 59 (28), 67, 69, 70[4], 71, 79, 80[40], 81, 93[35], 95, 103, 115, 117, 118, 120, 128[29], 129, 130[15]

NAi Publishers would like to thank the following people for their great help:
Robbin van der Berg (Syngenta); Bryn Bowles (Harptree); Pat Burns (Chiltern); Gill Gerken (PanAmerican); Annemarieke Hooij (Visions); Lauw de Jager (Bulb'Argence); Irma Jansen (Sahin); Jos de Jong (Rijnbeek); Marilyn Keen (Thompson); Carmen Klinner (Benary); William Lohuis (CODA); Jos van Nuenen; Ralf Rendels (Nebelung); Kurt Reynolds (Goldsmith); Robert Sanders (Florensis); Rob van der Voort (Van Hemert)

NAi Publishers is an internationally orientated publisher specialized in developing, producing and distributing books on architecture, visual arts and related disciplines.
www.naipublishers.nl info@naipublishers.nl

It was not possible to find all the copyright holders of the illustrations used. Interested parties are requested to contact NAi Publishers, Mauritsweg 23, 3012 JR Rotterdam, The Netherlands.

Available in North, South and Central America through D.A.P./ Distributed Art Publishers Inc, 155 Sixth Avenue 2nd Floor, New York, NY 10013-1507, Tel 212 6271999, Fax 212 6279484.

Available in the United Kingdom and Ireland through Art Data, 12 Bell Industrial Estate, 50 Cunnington Street, London W4 5HB, Tel 208 7471061, Fax 208 7422319.

Printed and bound in Belgium
ISBN 978-90-5662-023-3
Cover: Cosmos atrosanguineus (Visions Pictures)